The Last American President

The Last American President

A Broken Man, a Corrupt Party, and a World on the Brink

Thom Hartmann

BK®

Berrett–Koehler Publishers, Inc.

Berrett-Koehler Publishers, Inc.
1333 Broadway, Suite P100
Oakland, CA 94612–1921
Tel: (510) 817-2277
Fax: (510) 817-2278
bkconnection.com

ORDERING INFORMATION

Quantity sales. Special discounts are available on quantity purchases by corporations, associations, and others. For details, please go to bkconnection.com to see our bulk discounts or contact bookorders@bkpub.com for more information.

Individual sales. Berrett-Koehler publications are available through most bookstores. They can also be ordered directly from Berrett-Koehler: Tel: (800) 929-2929; Fax: (802) 864-7626; bkconnection.com.

Orders for college textbook / course adoption use. Please contact Berrett-Koehler: Tel: (800) 929-2929; Fax: (802) 864-7626.

Distributed to the US trade and internationally by Penguin Random House Publisher Services.

The authorized representative in the EU for product safety and compliance is EU Compliance Partner, Pärnu mnt. 139b-14, 11317 Tallinn, Estonia, www.eucompliancepartner.com, +372 5368 65 02.

Berrett-Koehler and the BK logo are registered trademarks of Berrett-Koehler Publishers, Inc.

Printed in the United States of America

Berrett-Koehler books are printed on long-lasting acid-free paper. When it is available, we choose paper that has been manufactured by environmentally responsible processes. These may include using trees grown in sustainable forests, incorporating recycled paper, minimizing chlorine in bleaching, or recycling the energy produced at the paper mill.

Library of Congress Control Number: 2025939444
The following is for reference only: ISBN 9798890571847 (paperback) | ISBN 9798890571854 (pdf) | ISBN 9798890571861 (epub)

First Edition

33 32 31 30 29 28 27 26 25   10 9 8 7 6 5 4 3 2 1

Book production: Susan Geraghty
Cover design: Ashley Ingram

To Louise Hartmann, without whom this book wouldn't exist.

Contents

The Last American President

Introduction

The End Begins with a Smile

The ignorance of one voter in a democracy impairs the security of all. —John F. Kennedy

IT DIDN'T LOOK LIKE THE END OF DEMOCRACY. IT LOOKED LIKE A TUESDAY. I remember watching the television that day, January 6, 2021, as a man stood on the Capitol lawn. Red hat, blank expression, that thousand-yard stare people get when something fundamental breaks inside them. His face was flushed crimson against the winter cold, fists clenched like he was holding onto the last threads of a reality rapidly unraveling, and his voice—already sandpaper-rough from hours of shouting—cracked as he howled into the January wind: "They're stealing my country!"[1]

Inside those historic halls, American police officers were being beaten with the very flagpoles that once carried our stars and stripes.[2] Outside, thousands swarmed barricades, waving signs proclaiming "Jesus is My Savior, Trump is My President" and "1776," equating their insurrection with our founding revolution, a perversion of history so profound it leaves historians breathless.[3] A gallows stood erected on the lawn. Pipe bombs waited silently nearby.[4] And the president of the United States—the man who had sworn an oath to protect the Constitution against all enemies, foreign and domestic—watched it all unfold on television, doing nothing.[5]

But here's what we must understand: this didn't start with violence. It didn't begin with tanks rolling down Pennsylvania Avenue or emergency decrees or a midnight coup with generals in dark rooms. It began with something far more insidious. It began with a smile.

A familiar grin from behind a podium. A catchphrase designed in a marketing meeting: "Make America Great Again."[6] A seductive promise that only he—not we, not us, not our democratic institutions—only HE could fix what ailed America.[7] There was always that wink to the cameras as he mocked journalists doing their constitutional duty, as he demonized immigrants seeking the American promise, as he insisted he could never lose unless someone cheated, because losing would mean the system was rigged against him.[8] And when he did lose? He smiled again, and lied. A Big Lie that would have made Goebbels proud.[9]

The Pattern of Democratic Collapse

History doesn't end in a blaze of glory or even in tragedy. It ends in applause. We've conditioned ourselves to believe tyranny arrives with jackboots and blood-red banners, goose-stepping soldiers and midnight arrests. But in twenty-first century America, it arrived in a designer suit (however ill-fitting), a private branded plane, and a social media account with millions of followers. It came through legal loopholes identified by cynical attorneys and billionaires' checkbooks, riding the algorithms of outrage and our insatiable hunger for spectacle. It came packaged as entertainment.

The pattern is depressingly familiar to students of democratic collapse. In Weimar Germany, the Nazi Party never won an outright majority in free elections. Instead, conservative elites believed they could control Hitler, using his popular appeal while restraining his worst impulses. They were wrong.[10]

In Venezuela, Hugo Chávez came to power through democratic elections, then systematically dismantled democratic guardrails by packing courts, attacking the press, and eventually rewriting the constitution.[11] In Hungary today, Viktor Orbán maintains the outward appearance of democracy while controlling media, judiciary, and electoral systems so thoroughly that opposition becomes functionally impossible.[12]

In each case, democracy died not through military coups but through legal mechanisms, not in a single dramatic moment but through the accumulation of seemingly minor changes. The forms of democracy remained—elections still happened, courts still ruled, newspapers still printed—but the substance had been hollowed out, replaced by the raw exercise of power unconstrained by democratic accountability.[13]

This book isn't simply about Donald Trump. How could it be? He's merely the symptom, not the disease. This book examines the ecosystem that built him:

A father who taught him that domination was the only currency worth pursuing.[14]

A mentor—Roy Cohn—who showed him that shame was for the weak, and that attacking was always better than defending.[15]

A political party that traded two centuries of principles for four years of raw power.[16]

A donor class that used him as a wrecking ball to destroy the administrative state that had once kept their avarice in check.[17]

A media landscape that fatally mistook charisma for character, volume for vision, and ratings for responsibility.[18]

Trump didn't hijack the system. Let's be absolutely clear about this. He revealed it. He pulled back the curtain and showed us what had been growing in the dark for decades.[19]

Voices from the Brink

Shaye Moss, a Georgia election worker who counted ballots in 2020, received death threats so severe she needed police protection. "I've seen America at its worst," she testified to Congress, "but I never thought fellow Americans would threaten to kill me for counting votes."[20]

Dr. Anthony Fauci, America's top infectious disease expert, required round-the-clock security after recommending COVID-19 precautions based on medical evidence. "They know where my children work and live," he revealed, describing how former patients he'd treated for years suddenly branded him a "traitor" and "deep state" operative.[21]

Maria Caffrey, a climate scientist with the National Park Service, watched as her research on sea-level rise was systematically censored. When she refused to remove references to human causes of climate change, she lost her position. "They didn't disagree with our findings," she testified to Congress. "They erased them."[22]

These voices—the poll worker, the doctor, the scientist—are canaries in our democratic coal mine. When those who count votes, protect public health, and investigate scientific truth become targets rather than public servants, democracy gasps for air.

He was not a mistake or an anomaly. He was the system's reflection in gold-tinted glass, a product of Citizens United, gerrymandering, and propaganda channels masquerading as news.[23] He rose not in defiance of democracy, but through its loopholes and fractures, the very weaknesses the Founders warned us about but that we, in our complacency, allowed to fester.[24]

And if he takes America down into the darkness of authoritarianism, it will not be an aberration. It will be a completion.

The completion of a Supreme Court reengineered to serve wealth rather than justice.[25]

The completion of a political party and media ecosystem organized around grievance and resentment instead of ideas and solutions.[26]

The completion of a public sphere so disillusioned it no longer believes in the possibility of a better future.[27]

The completion of a government so hollowed out by greed and rendered impotent by gridlock that it can no longer respond to crisis but only exploit it.[28]

This book is many things: a map of how we got here, a psychological autopsy of a broken man and the broken system that elevated him, a political reckoning long overdue, and most importantly, a warning.

It explains how America reached the brink not just of authoritarianism, but of irrelevance on the world stage. It reveals how one man, driven by ego and emptiness, was handed the nuclear codes by a party too cowardly and too compromised to stop him. And it examines what happens when the most powerful nation on Earth becomes effectively ungoverned when it trades empathy for vengeance, competence for chaos, and reality for ratings.[29]

We are not guaranteed another free election. The Constitution is not self-executing; it requires people of good faith to defend it.[30] We are not promised a second chance at this experiment called democracy.

This is potentially the story of the last president we may ever elect freely. Unless we choose to fight. Unless we recognize that democracy isn't something we have, it's something we do, every single day.

The choice, as it has always been in America, is ours.

The Making of Donald Trump

The Beginning: The Man Who Would Break America

Nearly all men can stand adversity, but if you want to test a man's character, give him power. —Abraham Lincoln

In the late 1960s, while working as a DJ and news reporter at WITL radio in Lansing, Michigan, I saw firsthand how a democratic government can rapidly erode when it's corrupted by official lies. As a teenager who'd been expelled from high school for starting an anti–Vietnam War newspaper, and then a member of Students for a Democratic Society at Michigan State University, I was subjected to police surveillance and arrest, experiences that to this day color my understanding of government.

Which is why when Louise and I watched the Confederate flag being paraded through the US Capitol on January 6, 2021, I felt a chill. This wasn't just an insurrection; it was the culmination of institutional erosion I've documented for decades on my radio show and in my books, beginning with Johnson and Nixon during the Vietnam era.

Democracies don't typically die suddenly. They erode gradually, their foundations weakened by corruption, the predations of the morbidly rich, and the systematic dismantling of institutional safeguards.

America didn't stumble into this Trump-driven crisis by accident. We were led here step by methodical step, with Donald Trump serving as an accelerant of institutional decay that began long before he entered politics in 2015.

To truly understand how a 246-year-old democracy could find itself on the brink of fascism, we must first understand the man who pushed it to the edge; not because he's uniquely brilliant or powerful, but because his particular pathologies perfectly matched the vulnerabilities in our system. Trump's lifelong patterns—his craving for dominance, his imperviousness to shame, his transactional notion of human relationships— became America's crisis once they were amplified by presidential power.

In the chapters that follow, I trace the formation of a dangerous demagogue through three critical stages. First, we'll return to that mansion in Queens, New York, where Fred Trump created a son incapable of empathy but desperate for validation, teaching young Donald that winning justified any means. Then we'll examine how Roy Cohn—one of America's most notorious political operatives—transformed Trump's raw narcissism into tactical weaponry, training him to attack, never apologize, manipulate media, and treat the legal system as a weapon for personal vengeance rather than justice. Finally, we'll see how Trump constructed a golden façade of success that masked decades of spectacular business failures, convincing millions he was qualified to lead the world's most powerful nation despite decades of evidence to the contrary.

This isn't just Trump's personal story. It's the chronicle of how America's elites—bankers, media executives, political strategists—repeatedly enabled and profited from a man they knew to be dangerous. The Trump we see today wasn't born; he was made, not just by family dysfunction but by systems that rewarded his worst impulses.

I've spent much of my life studying the intersection of power, psychology, and democracy's fragility. What we're witnessing isn't unprecedented in global history, but it is unparalleled in American experience. With these insights into the making of Donald Trump, we begin to understand how democracies fall and, perhaps, how ours might still be saved.

Because this isn't just about one twisted man. It's about whether the American experiment can survive the forces he unleashed.

CHAPTER 1

Queens, Cruelty, and Fred Trump

It is easier to build strong children than to repair broken men.
—Frederick Douglass

WHAT IF THE MOST DANGEROUS MAN IN THE WORLD WASN'T BORN A monster but was made one, in a mansion ruled by silence, fear, and cold ambition?

It was January 6, 2021, and Louise and I watched on CNN, mesmerized, as the Capitol of America was aflame with violence.

The marble halls of the Capitol, once symbols of democratic permanence, echoed with the sounds of shattering glass and enraged voices. Confederate flags—banners of treason that never made it inside the building during the Civil War—were being paraded past statues of Lincoln and Frederick Douglass. Police officers were beaten with the very flagpoles that moments earlier had flown the American flag. A gallows stood erected on the lawn, a noose swinging in the winter wind. And in the White House, just blocks away, the president of the United States watched it all unfold on television not with horror, but with fascination and satisfaction.[1]

Some asked how we got here; it was certainly a common question on my radio show in the following weeks. But the wiser question is: why didn't we see it coming?

To understand Donald Trump—to truly comprehend how a reality TV host and failed casino magnate could bring the world's oldest continuous democracy to the brink of collapse—we must go back to where it all began. Not to the golden escalator in 2015. Not to *The Apprentice* in 2004. Not even to his first bankruptcy or his first full-page newspaper ad calling for the execution of the wrongfully accused Central Park Five.[2]

We must return to a mansion in Queens. To a father who believed kindness was weakness. To a home that punished softness, grace, and

7

generosity. To the childhood that created a president unburdened by conscience.

Because Donald Trump wasn't born dangerous. He was shaped into a weapon by family, by mentors, and eventually by a political system too broken and too corrupted by money to stop him.

The Fortress in Jamaica Estates

Donald John Trump was born on June 14, 1946, the fourth of five children to Fred C. Trump and Mary Anne MacLeod Trump. Their home in Jamaica Estates, an exclusively (by law at the time) white enclave in Queens, was a twenty-three-room Tudor mansion, complete with imposing façade and coldly opulent interiors.[3] It stood as both symbol and incubator for the Trump family ethos: success measured in dollars and dominance, emotions seen as weakness, empathy dismissed as naïveté.

Fred Trump was not merely a successful businessman; he was a man whose worldview had been shaped by the Great Depression and who had clawed his way to wealth through a combination of tenacity, opportunism, and a willingness to skirt laws when they proved inconvenient to his ambitions.[4]

The Federal Housing Administration had been created in the 1930s under Roosevelt to make home ownership possible for ordinary Americans, but Fred Trump saw it primarily as an opportunity for personal enrichment. He built government-backed housing projects, cutting corners on construction while maximizing profits, practices that would eventually lead to investigations and hearings before the US Senate Banking Committee in 1954.[5]

Fred's approach to business mirrored his approach to parenting: extract maximum value, show no weakness, and win at all costs. He was a man who viewed kindness as a liability, emotions as indulgences, and his children as extensions of himself, measured not by their character or compassion, but by their ability to dominate others financially and psychologically.[6]

"He believed the world was filled with predators and prey—and only the ruthless would survive," recalled Donald's niece, Dr. Mary Trump, a clinical psychologist who later wrote that Fred was a "high-functioning sociopath" whose emotional absence and relentless focus on success created a toxic environment for his children. In her book *Too Much and Never*

Enough, she described how her uncle Donald's personality was formed in response to this emotional desert—his grandiosity, his need for constant validation, his inability to admit mistakes, and his casual cruelty all adaptive responses to a father who viewed vulnerability as unforgivable weakness.[7]

Fred would tell his children—particularly his sons—"You are a killer. . . . You are a king."[8] These weren't casual encouragements. They were imperatives. In the Trump household, success wasn't measured in happiness or fulfillment or contribution to community. It was measured in headlines, in square footage, in defeating others. And, even more gruesomely, it was zero-sum: for you to win, someone else had to lose.

Win-win was a totally alien concept in the Trump household, as we can see in Donald's inability to work with other nations today. In his mind, you either dominate or are dominated. Everything is hierarchy. And whoever's willing to be the most brutal must be the top dog.

Young Donald absorbed these lessons at his father's knee: rules were for the weak, for the "losers" who lacked the wit and will to bend them to their advantage. Money wasn't just wealth; it was a scoreboard. And people—especially those with less power—were either useful or obstacles.[9]

A Mother's Silence

While Fred dominated the household, Mary Anne MacLeod Trump played the role of an elegant but distant presence—one young Donald desperately tried to impress but rarely reached.[10]

She had come to the United States from Scotland as a teenager, fleeing poverty and hoping to build a life in New York. But after giving birth to her fifth child, she suffered serious medical complications, including hemorrhaging and infection, that left her ill for years. According to family accounts, she withdrew emotionally from her children, leaving the heavy lifting of parenting—and disciplining—to Fred.[11]

Mary Trump describes her grandmother as "neurotic and self-involved," noting that Donald received little comfort or maternal affection during his formative years. This maternal absence, combined with Fred's emotional detachment, created a household atmosphere that valued superficial strength over authentic connection.[12]

The Trump children competed fiercely for their father's limited approval, and Donald quickly learned that audacity, aggression, and an absolute refusal to acknowledge failure were the currencies that earned Fred's respect. Trump's older brother, Fred Jr., took a different path, pursuing interests that did not align with their father's vision. The elder Fred's treatment of his namesake son was a lesson in itself: Fred Jr.'s gentler nature and lack of interest in the real estate business were treated as moral failings rather than personal choices.[13]

When alcoholism eventually overtook Fred Jr., leading to his death at age forty-two, the family's response was not compassion but judgment. Donald would later cite his brother's fate as the reason he abstained from alcohol, but the deeper lesson he seemed to take was not about the dangers of addiction but about the price of failing to embody Fred Trump's ruthless values.[14]

Weakness is fatal, Donald concluded—a lesson that would shape his worldview for decades to come and eventually, catastrophically, inform his governing philosophy.[15]

A Childhood Marked by Discipline

This family dynamic was playing out against the backdrop of a changing America. The 1950s and 1960s, when Donald was coming of age, were decades of profound social transformation. The civil rights movement was challenging long-established racial hierarchies. The feminist movement was beginning to question traditional gender roles. The counterculture was rejecting materialism and militarism in favor of peace and communal values.

I saw this in my own family, having grown up in the same era. My "Eisenhower Republican" father, who saw Barry Goldwater as a hero (we campaigned door-to-door for him when I was thirteen in 1964), walked a neighborhood girl down the aisle when her father refused to because she was marrying a Black man. He printed on his mimeo machine the underground 'zine that got me kicked out of high school (a blessing that got me into college at sixteen) and defended me when I was arrested for protesting the Vietnam War, which he supported.

But inside the Trump mansion in Queens, time stood still. The values remained those of acquisition, dominance, and zero-sum competition. The outside world might be evolving toward greater equality and social justice, but in the Trump household, might still made right.[16]

Fred Trump's real estate empire was built in part on racial exclusion. In 1973, the Justice Department sued Trump Management for discriminating against Black rental applicants, a case that was eventually settled with a consent decree. Donald, who by then had joined his father's business, was named as a defendant alongside Fred. The tactics employed were not subtle: Black applicants would be told no apartments were available, while white applicants visiting the same buildings on the same day would be shown multiple options.[17]

This early exposure to racial discrimination as business practice cannot be overstated in its importance to understanding Donald Trump's later political strategy. He learned not just that racism could be profitable, but that when confronted with evidence of wrongdoing, the best defense was a good offense: deny everything, countersue, claim persecution, and never, under any circumstances, admit fault or express remorse.[18]

From an early age, Donald exhibited behavior that challenged authority and sought attention. His antics at the Kew-Forest School in Queens included bullying peers and defying teachers. At the age of thirteen, after numerous disciplinary issues, Fred decided to send Donald to the New York Military Academy (NYMA), hoping that the structured environment would instill discipline.[19]

To Donald, however, this wasn't just parental guidance. It was rejection, a father saying, "You are too much trouble, so I'm sending you away." And rather than learning empathy or consideration for others, Donald took a different lesson: the way to succeed wasn't to cooperate or show kindness, but to dominate within whatever system you found yourself.[20]

At NYMA, Trump found an environment that in many ways reinforced the hierarchical thinking he had absorbed at home. The military structure provided clear rankings, opportunities for visible achievement through promotions, and a value system that rewarded conformity to certain behavioral codes while encouraging competition for status. Trump thrived in this environment in some ways, earning athletic honors and rising to a leadership position as a student officer. But even here, his need to dominate led to problems; he was demoted from his position for hazing younger cadets, revealing an early pattern of abusing power when it was granted to him.[21]

This pattern would repeat throughout Trump's life: an ability to initially impress authority figures and gain positions of power, followed by abuses of that power that would eventually lead to downfall, only to begin the cycle again in a new arena. What never changed was Trump's conviction, instilled by Fred, that perception was more important than reality, that "winning" was the only value that mattered, and that admitting error was an unforgivable sign of weakness.[22]

The Lessons of a Real Estate Empire

When Trump moved beyond the relatively controlled environments of home and military school into the broader world, first as a student at Fordham University and later at the Wharton School of the University of Pennsylvania, the values he had internalized came with him. Though he would later boast of being a "brilliant student" at Wharton, contemporaries remember him differently: as academically unremarkable, more interested in his weekend trips to New York to work with his father than in engaging with ideas or broadening his intellectual horizons.[23]

What Trump was studying, more diligently than any academic subject, was his father's business model. After all, it's hard to underestimate the power of a parental role model, both in shaping worldview and teaching skills.

When I was around ten years old, my father and his best friend, Jerry Miller, started a vitamin company in our basement, buying a high-quality custom-made multivitamin in bulk that I and my brothers helped package into bottles with customized "Millhart Laboratories" labels. Dad and Jerry were adamant that their product was one of the best on the market, with a fierce pride in both the quality and integrity of their venture.

While the company never took off, I learned from my father how to be an entrepreneur, a lesson that led me to create five successful (and two unsuccessful) multimillion-dollar businesses as well as a residential treatment facility for abused children and, most recently, a national radio/TV program.

Unlike my dad, though, Fred Trump had built his fortune not

primarily through brilliant innovation or exceptional quality, but through political connections, aggressive self-promotion, creative accounting, and the exploitation of government programs meant to serve the public good. He cultivated relationships with Brooklyn's Democratic machine politicians, whose help he needed for zoning changes and building permits. He became adept at finding ways to extract maximum government subsidies for his projects while minimizing his tax liabilities.[24]

Most importantly, Fred understood the power of perception. Though his business was solidly middle-class housing, he presented himself as a developer of luxury properties, understanding that the appearance of success was often more valuable than success itself in attracting investors, placating lenders, and intimidating competitors. This lesson in the power of inflated claims and strategic hyperbole would become central to Donald Trump's later business and political strategy.[25]

Fred's impact on Donald extended beyond childhood. In the business realm, Fred served as both a mentor and a financial backer. He provided Donald with substantial loans and introduced him to key figures in the real estate industry. According to a *New York Times* Pulitzer Prize–winning investigation, Trump received at least $413 million (in 2018 dollars) from his father's empire, much of it through tax schemes that legal experts described as "improper" and in some cases outright "fraudulent."[26]

This financial safety net allowed Donald to take risks that other developers could not afford and to weather failures that would have bankrupted those who lacked his family backing. It also allowed him to maintain the image of success even during periods when his actual business performance was disastrous. The perception of success, cultivated through constant self-promotion and inflated claims about his wealth, became its own kind of currency, allowing him to continue attracting investors and lenders even as his actual track record raised serious questions.[27]

From Builder to Brand

By the 1980s, Trump had established himself not just as a real estate developer but as a brand, one built more on the perception of success than its reality. His 1987 book *The Art of the Deal*, ghostwritten by Tony Schwartz (who would later express deep regret for his role in creating the Trump mythology), presented a carefully curated version of Trump's business philosophy and personal narrative. The book, like much of Trump's self-presentation, emphasized his toughness, his instinctive brilliance, and his willingness to do whatever it took to win.[28]

"Most people are surprised by the way I work," Trump (or rather, Schwartz) wrote in *The Art of the Deal*. "I play it very loose. . . . I prefer to come to work each day and just see what develops." This seemingly casual approach to business decision-making would later find its parallel in Trump's approach to governance—reactive, impulsive, guided more by personal instinct and immediate self-interest than by strategic planning or coherent ideology.[29]

The book also revealed another aspect of Trump's psychology that would later prove significant: his zero-sum view of human interactions. "The final key to the way I promote is bravado," he wrote. "I play to people's fantasies. People may not always think big themselves, but they can still get very excited by those who do. That's why a little hyperbole never hurts. People want to believe that something is the biggest and the greatest and the most spectacular. I call it truthful hyperbole. It's an innocent form of exaggeration—and a very effective form of promotion."[30]

This passage is remarkable not just for its explicit acknowledgment of Trump's use of exaggeration as a marketing strategy, but for its framing of deception as "innocent" and its assumption that manipulating others' perceptions is a legitimate business tactic. The line between "truthful hyperbole" and outright lying would prove increasingly blurry as Trump's career progressed.

The Damage Done

Trump's first presidency revealed the full consequences of the worldview he developed under Fred's tutelage. The most damaging aspect wasn't his individual policy decisions or even his personal behavior, but the way he systematically undermined the institutional foundations of American democracy.

He attacked the independence of the judiciary, describing judges who ruled against his policies as biased or corrupt.[31] He politicized the Justice Department, pressuring it to investigate his political opponents and to go easy on his allies.[32] He undermined public trust in the electoral system, claiming without evidence that millions of illegal votes had been cast in the 2016 election and laying the groundwork for his later refusal to accept the results of the 2020 election.[33]

Trump's attacks on the media as "enemies of the people" echoed authoritarian rhetoric from some of history's darkest chapters.[34] His encouragement of violence against protesters at his rallies and his defense of white nationalists after the 2017 Charlottesville rally sent the message that certain types of political violence were acceptable.[35] His use of presidential pardons for political allies convicted of crimes committed on his behalf signaled that loyalty to him personally superseded obedience to the law.[36]

All of these actions reflected the worldview formed in that mansion in Queens, under the tutelage of a father who valued winning above all else and who saw rules as obstacles to be overcome rather than as the foundation of a functioning society. Trump brought to the presidency not just Fred's values but his methods: divide and conquer, use fear as motivation, reward loyalty, punish dissent, admit no error, and always, always attack rather than defend.[37]

The consequences would eventually culminate on January 6, 2021. As Louise and I watched the Capitol breach unfold on television, it was impossible not to see it as the logical endpoint of the child formed in that Queens mansion decades earlier: a psychology that viewed compromise as weakness, dominance as virtue, and rules as applying only to others.

This is how democracies die as we've seen over and over again across the world; not in a single blow, but through a million small corruptions, each one making the next easier, until the infrastructure of democracy has been hollowed out from within. It doesn't require tanks in the streets. It just requires a population willing to trade truth for tribal satisfaction, ethics for entertainment, and democracy for the promise of punishing their enemies.[38]

Fred Trump's most lasting legacy wasn't the buildings he constructed or the fortune he amassed. It was the belief system he instilled in his son, a system defined by its absence of empathy, its worship of dominance, and its view of human relationships as purely transactional.

The story that began in that mansion in Queens is still playing out before us. Donald Trump's psychology, shaped by a father who valued dominance over decency and perception over reality, continues to corrupt American politics in profound ways as he's now set out to fundamentally alter the nature of our American system of government.

This is the true danger: not just what Trump did, but what he made possible and is now doing.

Trump was never simply a personal anomaly. He was the product of systems: a family system that rewarded cruelty and punished empathy. A business system that valued perception over reality. A political system that had gradually surrendered to the power of money (largely as the result of a series of corrupt all-Republican-appointee Supreme Court decisions) and spectacle. A media system that prioritized outrage over truth. And a culture that had, in too many ways, confused the trappings of success with character.

Understanding how we arrived here is vital; it's the first, necessary step in preventing what could happen next. For unless we confront the damage already done—to our institutions, to our shared understanding of truth, and to our capacity for empathy and collective action—we may find ourselves not at the end of an aberrant presidency, but at the beginning of something far worse: an America where democracy survives in name only, while power flows unchecked to those willing to abandon all principle in its pursuit.

CHAPTER 2

Roy Cohn's Apprentice

Power is not what you have but what the enemy thinks you have.
—Saul Alinsky, *Rules for Radicals*

I WAS TWENTY-TWO IN 1973 AND HAD JUST STARTED AN HERBAL TEA COMpany when I became entranced by the business self-help movement. Louise and I listened to Earl Nightingale tapes in the car when we'd take weekend two-hour drives up to my grandparents' house in Newaygo, Michigan. I read books by Napoleon Hill (*Think and Grow Rich*) and Claude Bristol (*The Magic of Believing*) so many times I had entire sections memorized. I got a "pillow speaker" so I could go to sleep at night listening to their tapes.

W. Clement Stone, the insurance multimillionaire, had created a foundation that distributed posters and stickers with his slogans—"Do It Now!" and "Thinking will not overcome fear but action will!"—on them, and they decorated our apartment. I took the Dale Carnegie Course on public speaking, probably the best decision (outside of marrying Louise) of my life; it was transformational.

That was an era when many young people in business were looking for role models and mentors, a reboot of the 1930s when Norman Vincent Peale had electrified a generation of small-businesspeople with his books *The Art of Living* and *You Can Win*. My business mentor was a guy named Terry O'Connor who owned a small advertising agency in Lansing and took me under his wing; I learned a lot, we became lifetime friends, and we started two businesses that made us both a lot of money (and a third one that never really got going).

Donald Trump was, during that same time, also looking for a mentor, as his father was far too conventional and wed to his Queens properties for Donald's taste. So, before he had a movement, a base, or a party, Donald had Roy Cohn. And that was, for him, more than enough.

It was 1973, and the Trump real estate empire faced its first major crisis. The Justice Department had filed a lawsuit against Donald Trump, his father Fred, and their company, charging them with systemic discrimination against Black renters, a serious allegation that threatened not just their business but their carefully cultivated public image. Trump, then just twenty-seven years old and eager to establish himself in Manhattan, not just Queens, needed help.[1]

At Le Club, a Manhattan nightspot frequented by the city's power brokers, Trump was introduced to a forty-six-year-old attorney whose reputation preceded him—a man whose name had been infamous in American politics for two decades, whose tactics were feared, and whose absence of ethics was legendary.

Roy Marcus Cohn.

What happened next would transform not just Trump's approach to business and, eventually, politics, but the very character of American public life. For in Roy Cohn, Donald Trump found more than just a lawyer. He found a template, a model for how to wield power ruthlessly, how to manipulate media shamelessly, and how to crush opponents mercilessly.[2]

If Donald Trump is the political id of twenty-first-century America—rageful, shameless, and obsessed with dominance—then Roy Cohn was his emotional blueprint and strategic godfather. Every autocrat has a tutor. Every bully, a coach. For Trump, that man was Roy Cohn: the disgraced former McCarthyite who taught him that lying was a strategy, lawsuits were weapons, and admitting fault was suicide.

Trump didn't just admire Roy Cohn. He absorbed him. And in doing so, he inherited a political playbook so effective and corrosive that it would one day redefine the Republican Party itself and bring American democracy to the brink of collapse.[3]

The Making of a Monster

By the time he met Donald Trump in 1973, Roy Cohn was already an infamous figure in American political history, a man whose name was synonymous with character assassination, reckless accusation, and ruthless pursuit of power at any cost.

Born to an affluent Jewish family in the Bronx in 1927, Cohn was a prodigy of sorts, entering Columbia Law School at just seventeen and becoming a prosecutor in the US Attorney's Office in Manhattan by twenty.[4] But it was his role in the 1951 espionage trial of Julius and Ethel Rosenberg that first brought him to national attention. As the assistant prosecutor, the twenty-four-year-old Cohn pushed aggressively for the death penalty, particularly for Ethel, despite substantial questions about the extent of her involvement in her husband's espionage. As Cohn would later boast in his autobiography, he had privately lobbied the judge for the death sentence, an extraordinary ethical breach for a prosecutor.[5]

Cohn's ruthlessness in the Rosenberg case revealed something fundamental about his character that would later resonate deeply with Trump: the belief that winning justifies any means. In his pursuit of the death penalty for Ethel Rosenberg—a mother of two young boys—Cohn manipulated evidence, pressured witnesses, and engaged in ex parte communications with the judge.[6]

Years later, declassified Soviet cables would show that while Julius Rosenberg was indeed a spy, the evidence against Ethel was much weaker. David Greenglass, Ethel's brother and the key witness against her, would eventually admit that he had lied in his testimony at Cohn's urging.[7] The execution of Ethel Rosenberg remains one of the most controversial judicial killings in American history (even my dad, the anti-communist Republican, was troubled by it), and Cohn's role in it established his willingness to destroy lives in service of his ambitions.

This early triumph caught the attention of Senator Joseph McCarthy, who made Cohn his chief counsel during the infamous anti-communist hearings of the early 1950s. Together, McCarthy and Cohn embarked on a campaign of accusation, innuendo, and character assassination that ruined countless lives and careers without ever uncovering a single Soviet spy.[8] Their tactics were as simple as they were devastating: make bold, inflammatory accusations; demand that the accused prove a negative; use the media to amplify fear; and never, ever back down from a claim, no matter how thoroughly debunked.

The hearings revealed another aspect of Cohn's character that would later influence Trump: his mastery of media manipulation. Cohn understood intuitively that appearance often matters more than reality, that bold assertions frequently override facts, and that the camera loves conflict and controversy. He staged the hearings as theater, complete with dramatic revelations, confrontational exchanges, and shocking accusations, all designed to create compelling television that would keep Americans fearful and McCarthy powerful.[9]

The McCarthy hearings finally collapsed in 1954 during the Army-McCarthy proceedings, when the Army's counsel Joseph Welch famously asked McCarthy, "Have you no sense of decency, sir? At long last, have you left no sense of decency?"[10] It was the beginning of the end for McCarthy, but not for Cohn. He resigned and retreated to New York, where he reinvented himself as a power broker and attorney for the city's elite—and its underworld. His client list eventually included Catholic Cardinal Francis Spellman, Yankees owner George Steinbrenner, the Roman Catholic Archdiocese of New York, and various mafia figures, including bosses Tony Salerno, Carmine Galante, and John Gotti.[11]

This ability to reinvent himself after catastrophic public failure would become another lesson Trump absorbed. Just as Cohn had transformed from disgraced McCarthy henchman to celebrated New York power broker, Trump would later reinvent himself repeatedly: from failed casino magnate to reality TV star, from bankrupt businessman to self-proclaimed billionaire, from tabloid joke to president of the United States. The key was never to acknowledge defeat, but to immediately claim a new victory.[12]

By the 1970s, Cohn had developed a reputation as a fixer who could make problems disappear, often through intimidation, threats, and his extensive connections within New York's judicial system and media. As his former law partner Tom Bolan once explained, "Roy's standard method was to attack, attack. Even when he was wrong, especially when he was wrong."[13]

It was this man—a master of ethical corruption and aggressive counterattack—who would become Donald Trump's most important mentor.

The Meeting of Minds

When Trump and Cohn first met at Le Club in 1973, Trump didn't just see a potential lawyer. He saw a kindred spirit. As Trump would later recount: "I knew that Roy was the right guy for me. . . . He was a genius.

He was a savage. He didn't care what anyone said about him. He would do anything to win."[14]

The meeting came at a critical juncture for the young Trump. At twenty-seven, he was eager to break out of his father's shadow and establish himself in Manhattan real estate—a world far more glamorous and prestigious than Fred Trump's outer-borough apartment buildings. But he faced a significant obstacle: the Justice Department lawsuit alleging racial discrimination in Trump properties.

The evidence was substantial: Black applicants were routinely turned away from Trump buildings or told no apartments were available, while white applicants were shown multiple options. Former employees testified about marking applications from Black renters with a "C" for "colored." Testers from the New York Urban League had documented the discrimination firsthand.[15]

For most defendants, especially those seeking to build a reputation in New York's high society, such allegations would have been cause for quiet settlement and reform. But Cohn saw an opportunity to teach his new protégé a different approach.

Cohn's advice on the Justice Department's housing discrimination lawsuit was simple and direct: Never settle. Counterattack. Sue the government for $100 million for defamation. Call the prosecutors racists themselves. According to Trump's own account, Cohn told him, "Tell them to go to hell and fight the thing in court and let them prove you discriminated."[16]

Trump followed Cohn's advice to the letter, holding a press conference to denounce the lawsuit as "outrageous." The Trump Organization filed a $100 million countersuit against the DOJ, a suit that was quickly dismissed by the court as frivolous. But the aggressive posture worked in the court of public opinion. After two years of legal battles, the case was settled with a consent decree in which the Trumps made no admission of guilt and committed to only nominal changes in their rental practices. Trump claimed victory, though, in reality, the case had revealed a pattern of racial discrimination that would continue in various forms throughout Trump's career.[17]

For Trump, however, the takeaway was clear: Cohn's approach— deny, attack, never admit fault—was effective. It was the beginning of a relationship that would last more than a decade, with Cohn serving as Trump's lawyer, fixer, media handler, and most importantly, his tutor in the dark arts of power and manipulation.[18]

The relationship between Trump and Cohn quickly deepened beyond the professional. Trump became a fixture at Cohn's lavish dinner parties at his townhouse on East 68th Street, where politicians, judges, mobsters, and celebrities mingled freely. Through Cohn, Trump gained access to a world of power and connection that would prove invaluable to his ambitions. Cohn introduced Trump to political fixers like Roger Stone and media power brokers like Rupert Murdoch, relationships that would later prove crucial to Trump's political ascent.[19]

For his part, Cohn found in Trump an eager student, someone with the wealth, ambition, and moral flexibility to fully implement his philosophy. As journalist Ken Auletta observed after watching the two men interact at numerous social events: "There was something almost paternal in how Roy treated Donald. He was molding him, and Trump was drinking it all in."[20]

The Cohn Doctrine

What did Donald Trump learn from Roy Cohn? The lessons were as simple as they were poisonous:

First, never apologize or admit wrongdoing, ever. Cohn viewed contrition as weakness and would rather die (literally, as it turned out) than acknowledge error or fault. As journalist Ken Auletta, who covered Cohn extensively, noted, "The idea that you can admit a mistake is not part of Roy's genetic code."[21] This principle would become so fundamental to Trump's approach that even faced with irrefutable evidence—a recorded confession of sexual assault on the *Access Hollywood* tape, for instance—he would deny, deflect, and attack rather than offer the slightest acknowledgment of impropriety.[22]

Second, always counterattack, and always with greater force than you received. When criticized or accused, Cohn's response was invariably to hit back harder, to escalate, to make the accuser regret ever mentioning his name. As Cohn himself explained to a reporter: "I bring out the worst in my enemies, and that's how I get them to defeat themselves."[23]

This tactic became Trump's signature move, whether attacking Gold Star parents who criticized him, mocking a disabled reporter who questioned his claims, or threatening critics with lawsuits and retribution.[24]

Third, use the legal system as a weapon, not a recourse for justice. Cohn taught Trump that lawsuits were instruments of intimidation, not vehicles for dispute resolution. He filed cases not to win—though winning was nice—but to punish, to harass, and to silence. The expense and stress of litigation was the point, not the legal outcome. Trump would eventually be involved in over 3,500 lawsuits—an unprecedented number for any American businessperson or politician—using the courts not to seek justice but to exhaust opponents with fewer resources.[25]

Fourth, manipulate the media ruthlessly. Cohn was a master at planting stories, cultivating journalists, and creating controversy to serve his ends. He understood that perception trumped reality, that bold claims often went unchallenged, and that most people would remember the accusation but not the retraction.[26] Trump elevated this approach to an art form, calling reporters using pseudonyms like "John Barron" to plant favorable stories about himself, staging pseudo-events to attract coverage, and later, using Twitter to bypass media filters entirely and inject his unfiltered messages directly into the public consciousness.[27]

Fifth, use fear as both shield and sword. Cohn understood that people who are afraid—of communists, of crime, of social change, of the "other"—are easier to manipulate and more willing to accept authoritarian solutions. He helped McCarthy weaponize the Red Scare, stoking paranoia about secret communists undermining America from within.[28] Trump would adapt this tactic to the twenty-first century, stoking fears about immigrants, Muslims, "inner city" crime, and later, a "deep state" conspiracy, always positioning himself as the only solution to these terrifying threats.[29]

Finally, build a fortress of loyalty around yourself. Cohn demanded absolute devotion from his clients and associates, and he repaid it in kind, at least until they were no longer useful. He created a network of mutual obligation and fear that served as both sword and shield in his battles.[30] Trump's infamous demand for loyalty—from James Comey, from his cabinet members, from Republican legislators—and his swift punishment of perceived disloyalty, all echo Cohn's approach to power.[31]

Trump absorbed these lessons like a sponge. As journalist Wayne Barrett, who covered Trump for decades, observed: "Cohn's philosophy shaped the real estate developer's worldview and the belligerent public persona visible in Trump's presidential campaign."[32]

The evidence of Cohn's influence is everywhere in Trump's subsequent career. The constant lawsuits against journalists, critics, and former associates. The reflexive counterpunching. The use of nondisclosure agreements and threats. The demand for loyalty. The refusal—ever—to acknowledge error or defeat. Each is a page torn directly from Cohn's playbook.[33]

But perhaps the most important lesson Trump learned from Cohn was the most dangerous: that institutions can be bent and broken if one is shameless enough, aggressive enough, and persistent enough. Cohn had repeatedly violated legal ethics, manipulated the press, corrupted judges, and intimidated witnesses—all while maintaining his position as a respected (if feared) member of New York society.[34] Trump observed that the safeguards designed to protect democracy and ensure accountability—the courts, the press, regulatory agencies, ethical norms—were far more vulnerable than they appeared, especially when confronted with someone willing to attack them relentlessly and without shame.[35]

The End of the Relationship, but Not the Influence

By the mid-1980s, Cohn's health was failing. His legal career was collapsing as well: he had been the subject of numerous disciplinary proceedings and was eventually disbarred in 1986 for "dishonesty, fraud, deceit, and misrepresentation."[36]

As Cohn approached death, Trump began to distance himself. The pattern would become familiar in Trump's later life; the discarding of associates who could no longer serve his purposes. According to Roger Stone, a mutual associate: "When Roy got sick, Donald dropped him like a hot potato."[37]

The final betrayal was particularly cruel. When Cohn was diagnosed with AIDS—a condition he denied to the end, insisting he had liver cancer—he reached out to Trump for support. Cohn had, after all, been Trump's most important mentor, had guided his entry into Manhattan real estate, had protected him from the DOJ, had connected him with power-ful figures who advanced his career. But Trump, sensing that Cohn was no longer useful and potentially a liability, distanced himself. When Cohn called asking Trump to find him a room at one of his hotels where he could recover, Trump reportedly promised to help but never called back.[38]

Cohn's final months were a stark illustration of the transactional worldview he had helped instill in Trump. As Cohn lay dying, many of his former clients and associates abandoned him, not just because of his illness, but because his power was gone. In the world Cohn had con-structed, where relationships were based on utility rather than loyalty or affection, his declining health rendered him worthless. It was the logical endpoint of the philosophy he had lived by and taught to Trump: people matter only to the extent they can serve your interests. When they can no longer do so, they are discarded.[39]

When Cohn died in August 1986, Trump was not among the mourn-ers at his funeral. But the lessons Cohn had taught him—the tactics, the worldview, the absolute commitment to winning at all costs—remained. Trump had not just hired Cohn; he had internalized him. And the influ-ence of that relationship would extend far beyond Atlantic City or Man-hattan real estate.[40]

It would, in time, shape the American presidency itself.

"Where's My Roy Cohn?"

In 2018, as the Russia investigation intensified and legal troubles mounted, President Trump reportedly slammed the table in the Oval Office and demanded: "Where's my Roy Cohn?"[41]

The question revealed more than just Trump's frustration with his then-Attorney General Jeff Sessions. It revealed the entire template for his view of the Justice Department, of law enforcement, of the very concept of rule of law. In Trump's mind, shaped by Cohn's toxic tutelage, the attor-ney general was not the nation's chief law enforcement officer, bound by constitutional oath and legal ethics. He was the president's personal fixer, his attack dog, his protector.[42]

This view—profoundly anti-democratic and fundamentally corrupt—permeated the first Trump presidency. William Barr's misleading summary of the Mueller Report, the firing of US attorneys investigating Trump associates, the persistent attacks on "disloyal" FBI officials, the dangling of pardons to silence potential witnesses: each echoed Cohn's approach to legal institutions as tools of personal power rather than guardrails for democratic governance.[43]

The Trump years didn't just damage American institutions. They exposed their vulnerability to a president willing to deploy Roy Cohn's tactics from the Oval Office. And they revealed how quickly democratic norms and constitutional safeguards can crumble when confronted with a leader who refuses to acknowledge their legitimacy or accept their constraints.[44]

In the end, Roy Cohn's lasting legacy wasn't just his influence on Donald Trump. It was his demonstration of how American democracy could be attacked, not from outside, but from within, using the very tools and institutions designed to protect it as weapons to undermine it. Trump simply took the Cohn playbook and scaled it to national proportions.

And we're still living with the consequences.[45]

CHAPTER 3

The Mask of Success

We are what we pretend to be, so we must be careful about what we pretend to be. —Kurt Vonnegut, *Mother Night*

WHAT IF THE MOST POWERFUL MAN IN THE WORLD BUILT HIS EMPIRE NOT on success, but on pretending he had it?

I remember September 11, 2023. It wasn't just the anniversary of 9/11; there was also a grim (but, frankly, satisfying) show going on in Manhattan that had the nation (and Louise, me, and the listeners to my radio program) glued to their TV screens.

In a crowded federal courthouse in New York City, former president Donald Trump sat stone-faced as his former accountant testified under oath about the Trump Organization's financial statements. For decades, Allen Weisselberg explained, the company routinely inflated Trump's assets—sometimes by billions of dollars—to secure loans, insurance, and business opportunities. Properties were suddenly worth double on paper. Apartment buildings grew fictional floors. Golf courses sprouted imaginary mansions ready for sale.

It was, the accountant admitted, a systematic campaign of deception designed to make Trump appear far wealthier and more successful than he actually was.[1]

Just days earlier, Trump had launched his campaign to recapture the presidency in 2024, once again promising voters that only he—the self-proclaimed business genius—could fix America's economy. "I'm the only president in modern history who left office with a smaller national debt than when I came into office," he declared at a rally, a claim so brazenly false that even Fox News felt compelled to correct it. During Trump's presidency, the national debt had actually increased by $7.8 trillion, nearly 40 percent and more than any other president in history.[2]

These courthouse revelations surprised no one who'd been paying attention. They were merely the latest documented evidence of what had been apparent throughout Trump's career: his business empire was never built on success. It was built on the *appearance* of success, a golden façade carefully constructed through media manipulation, aggressive self-promotion, and outright fraud.

It's a façade that didn't just make Trump wealthy and famous, it made him president. And it's a façade that continues to threaten American democracy itself as he has again returned to power.

Born on Third Base, Claimed He Hit a Home Run

In American mythology, few archetypes are more powerful than the self-made man. I was so entranced with the idea that I started my first business—fixing TVs in my neighborhood in Lansing—when I was thirteen years old and had just gotten my amateur radio license . . . and went on to being a serial entrepreneur through my entire life. (I haven't had a "job" since I was a DJ and later news reporter for WITL AM-FM when I was sixteen and living on my own.)

From Benjamin Franklin to Andrew Carnegie to Steve Jobs, we celebrate those who, through determination and ingenuity, rise from modest beginnings to extraordinary success. It's the story that makes America itself possible, that here, unlike the aristocracies of the Old World, merit matters more than bloodline.

Like me and my wannabe entrepreneur father, Donald Trump understood the power of this narrative, although he played it out on a much larger (and less ethical) stage.

Throughout his career, Trump positioned himself as a self-made billionaire, a bootstrapper who, with a "small loan of a million dollars" from his father, built a global empire through his own brilliance and hustle. The origin story he told the world—and himself—was one of overcoming obstacles, conquering New York's brutal real estate market through grit, vision, and unparalleled deal-making skill.

It was, like so much about Trump, a performance masking a very different reality.

According to a *New York Times* Pulitzer Prize–winning investigation in 2018, Trump received at least $413 million in today's dollars from his father, Fred, not the $1 million "small loan" he repeatedly claimed. The investigation, based on more than one hundred thousand pages of financial documents, revealed that "the president has often sold himself as a self-made billionaire, but a *Times* investigation found that he received at least $413 million from his father's real estate empire, much of it through tax dodges in the 1990s."[3]

The mechanisms of this wealth transfer were elaborate and, in many cases, potentially fraudulent. The *Times* documented how Fred Trump created numerous shell companies to disguise gifts to his children. In one particularly brazen scheme, a company called "All County Building Supply & Maintenance" was established as a purchasing agent for Fred Trump's properties. In reality, it was a vehicle for transferring wealth to Donald and his siblings while simultaneously defrauding tenants in rent-controlled buildings.[4]

As David Cay Johnston, who won a Pulitzer Prize for his reporting on tax loopholes for the wealthy, observed: "Donald Trump is not a self-made man. He is a self-made myth."[5]

Trump didn't earn his fortune. He inherited it. And then lied about it.

The Emperor of Bankruptcy

When I was seventeen, I started a small electronics business in East Lansing across the street from MSU, growing it to five employees (including Louise, who did the bookkeeping). It was called The Electronics Joint and our logo was a pot cigarette (a "joint") with rabbit ears antenna on top. But I expanded the business too fast, and within three years had managed to drive it into bankruptcy.

It was one of the best lessons of my life, and while a few other businesses I started didn't take off, I never repeated that mistake of borrowing money to grow a business faster than the market itself could provide. Donald Trump, by contrast, never learned the same lesson, even though he had multiple chances.

Between 1991 and 2009, Trump filed for corporate bankruptcy six times—an unprecedented record for a major American business figure. His failures included the Trump Taj Mahal (1991), Trump Plaza Hotel and Casino (1992), Trump Castle Casino Resort (1992), the Plaza Hotel in New York (1992), Trump Hotels & Casino Resorts (2004), and Trump Entertainment Resorts (2009).[6]

The pattern was consistent. Trump would secure financing for grandiose projects, often by personally guaranteeing portions of the loans. He would launch with enormous fanfare and self-celebration. Then reality—in the form of mismanagement, market downturns, or simple mathematical impossibility—would set in. The businesses would collapse, investors would lose billions, but Trump himself would emerge remarkably unscathed (unlike my business crash in 1970; I eventually paid back all my creditors), protected by corporate structures that insulated his personal wealth from his business failures.

But Trump's failures weren't victimless. The real casualties were the small businesses caught in his wake. J. Michael Diehl, who sold Trump $100,000 worth of pianos for the Taj Mahal, was eventually forced to accept seventy cents on the dollar, a $30,000 loss that threatened his small business. "I feel like I've been taken by the best," Diehl later told reporters. "He knew what he was doing, and he did it intentionally."[7]

USA Today identified at least sixty lawsuits by ordinary Americans—carpenters, painters, glass companies, even a toilet manufacturer—who claimed Trump had refused to pay them for their work.[8] For these contractors, it wasn't just business. It was economic violence.

I've spent my entire life in an entrepreneurial space, and even cofounded a group for entrepreneurs in Atlanta that's still around (the "Terminus Group"); we'd get together once a month in a private room in a nice restaurant and swap stories, share successes and failures, and mentor and support each other. Never in all those fifty-plus years in business (including my being profiled on the front page of the *Wall Street Journal* and in an editorial and book by the publisher/editor of *Inc. Magazine*) have I known a single businessperson who delighted in screwing vendors, contractors, or employees.

Frankly, I suspect most businesspeople would recoil from such a person, viewing him as a predator to be avoided. Which, it turns out, perfectly describes Donald Trump.

Trump Steaks, Trump Vodka, Trump University

As Trump's ability to secure financing for major construction projects diminished following his multiple bankruptcies, he pivoted to a new business model: selling not buildings, but his name. By the 2000s, Trump had essentially transformed from a builder to a brand.

The results were a parade of failures that would have humbled a less narcissistic man:

- Trump Steaks were sold through Sharper Image, a store better known for massage chairs and electronic gadgets than quality meat. The venture lasted just two months in 2007. As Sharper Image CEO Jerry Levin later admitted: "We literally sold almost no steaks. If we sold $50,000 of steaks grand total, I'd be surprised."[9]

- Trump Vodka, launched in 2006 with the ridiculous tagline "Success Distilled," ceased production in 2011 after failing to gain traction in a competitive spirits market. Trump, a teetotaler, nonetheless proclaimed it would outsell Grey Goose. It didn't come close.

- Trump University represented perhaps the most egregious of Trump's failed ventures—not merely a business failure but an alleged criminal enterprise. Far from a university, it was an unaccredited series of seminars promising to teach Trump's real estate "secrets" to ordinary Americans. Students, many of them elderly or financially vulnerable, paid up to $35,000 for courses that former employees would later describe as a "fraudulent scheme" designed to "separate people from their money."[10] This led to multiple lawsuits alleging fraud, culminating in a $25 million settlement in 2018 that provided refunds to over six thousand former students.[11]

Each failure was brushed aside or reframed as a success, because Trump's business model wasn't about performance, it was about projection. The appearance of success mattered more than actual success. The gold-plated name was more valuable than the substandard product behind it. The press conference announcing the venture generated more value than the venture itself.

This was not success. It was the simulation of success, a simulation so convincing that even Trump himself seemed unable to distinguish between his mythology and reality.

The Invention of a Titan

In 1987, *The Art of the Deal* was published, a book that would cement Trump's image as a business genius in popular culture. The book was a runaway bestseller, spending forty-eight weeks on the *New York Times* bestseller list. Even Louise and I (then running an advertising agency in Atlanta with dozens of Fortune 500 companies as clients) read it at the time, and we both thought it was pretty good; everybody we knew in business was discussing it.

There was just one problem: Trump didn't write it. And according to the man who did, much of it wasn't true.

Tony Schwartz, the ghostwriter hired to craft Trump's business "memoir," spent eighteen months with Trump, attempting to extract something approaching a coherent philosophy from Trump's rambling self-aggrandizement. What he discovered was a man with "no attention span," who was fundamentally "insecure" and obsessed with public perception.

In a remarkable 2016 interview with the *New Yorker*, Schwartz expressed profound regret for his role in creating the Trump mythology: "I put lipstick on a pig. I feel a deep sense of remorse that I contributed to presenting Trump in a way that brought him wider attention and made him more appealing than he is."[12]

Schwartz revealed that the book's depiction of Trump as a brilliant dealmaker was largely fictional. Trump's supposed business philosophy—"truthful hyperbole" being perhaps the most famous concept—was crafted by Schwartz to put a positive spin on what was, in reality, compulsive lying. "'Truthful hyperbole' was my euphemism for a lie," Schwartz explained.[13]

Despite its questionable veracity, *The Art of the Deal* transformed Trump's public image. He was everywhere: *Oprah, Lifestyles of the Rich and Famous,* tabloid covers. The media, desperate for the spectacle Trump reliably provided, largely played along. Few journalists investigated whether Trump's claims about his wealth, his deals, or his business acumen were actually true.

By the early 2000s, Trump had pulled off a remarkable feat: his actual business record was one of repeated, spectacular failure, but his public image was that of the ultimate winner—the living embodiment of wealth, success, and the American dream.

The Apprentice: Image Becomes Identity

If *The Art of the Deal* laid the groundwork for Trump's business mythology, it was his next venture into media that would seal it permanently in the American consciousness: *The Apprentice*.

Premiering on NBC in January 2004, *The Apprentice* was the brainchild of producer Mark Burnett, who saw in Trump the perfect central figure for a reality show about business competition. The show was an immediate hit, drawing as many as twenty-eight million viewers for its first season finale. I watched a few episodes and found it formulaic and hokey, but Louise—like most of America—was entranced.

In her defense, she redeemed herself when we attended the 2011 White House Correspondent's Dinner where President Obama humorously peeled the bark off Trump. At the predinner party put on by the *Washington Post*, we were standing near the door to the ballroom when Trump, an attractive woman who may have been Melania (we didn't recognize her at the time), and his two bodyguards walked in.

Louise was standing about four feet from Donald and stared at his forehead; he seemed to think he was being admired, as he gave her a half-smile. She then turned to me and, in a loud voice, said, "Bad plugs!" Trump turned red, spun around, and left the room as the people around us chuckled. It really wasn't his night (although I've always thought it may have been his humiliation at the hands of Obama that night which spurred him to run for president).

But like *The Art of the Deal* before it, *The Apprentice* was a work of fiction. The boardroom where Trump rendered his famous verdicts wasn't his actual office but a set constructed for the show. The helicopter and limousine were props. The "jobs" offered to winners were often ceremonial positions created for the show rather than actual executive roles.[14]

Most significantly, the show portrayed Trump as the head of a thriving, expanding business empire at precisely the time when his actual business was in dire straits. By 2004, Trump had already declared corporate bankruptcy three times. His casino company, Trump Hotels & Casino Resorts, would declare bankruptcy for a fourth time that very year, with Trump resigning as CEO.[15]

What *The Apprentice* accomplished was remarkable: it transformed Trump from a tabloid figure associated with gaudy excess and business failure into an authoritative symbol of American business acumen. For the millions of Americans who watched the show, Trump wasn't the guy who stiffed contractors and bankrupted casinos. He was the billionaire boss who fired incompetence with flair.

It wasn't just that viewers believed the fictional portrayal of Trump. The fiction became, for all practical purposes, the reality. As Ivanka Trump told a documentary filmmaker in 2010: "Every article from then on out referred to him as 'billionaire Donald Trump.' Everything was billion, billion, billion. And I think that that did a tremendous thing for his brand and for his properties."[16]

Losing More Than Any American

If the mask of success Trump constructed through media manipulation was impressive, the reality it concealed was equally astonishing, but for very different reasons.

In May 2019, the *New York Times* published another bombshell investigation into Trump's finances. After obtaining printouts from Trump's official Internal Revenue Service tax transcripts from 1985 to 1994, journalists discovered a financial reality that completely contradicted Trump's carefully crafted public image.

The headline was stunning in its simplicity: "Decade in the Red: Trump Tax Figures Show over $1 Billion in Business Losses." The investigation revealed that "year after year, Mr. Trump appears to have lost more money than nearly any other individual American taxpayer."[17]

The numbers were staggering:

- 1985: Trump reported losses of $46.1 million from his core businesses.

- 1990 and 1991: Trump's losses exceeded $250 million each year.

- Total over ten years: $1.17 billion in losses.

These weren't just business setbacks. They represented a level of financial mismanagement so profound that Trump was losing more money than almost any other American taxpayer during this period. And yet, throughout these disastrous years, Trump was appearing on television, in magazines, and in newspapers as the very personification of business success. Behind the gold-plated façade, the reality was a businessman whose ventures regularly failed, who was kept afloat by his father's money, by banks too invested to let him fail, and eventually, by the licensing of his name to properties and products he neither built nor created.

The Brand That Became a Weapon

By 2015, when Trump descended the escalator in Trump Tower to announce his candidacy for president, he had transformed himself into a brand that millions trusted. Not for his policy knowledge. Not for his moral compass. But because he looked like a winner, and in an America increasingly disenchanted with political elites, looking like a winner was enough.

When mainstream journalists attempted to fact-check Trump's claims about his business record, his supporters dismissed these reports as "fake news" or attacks from a biased media. The decades-long investment in creating the Trump mythology had paid off; no amount of factual reporting could penetrate the image now firmly established in the public consciousness.

As linguist George Lakoff explained: "Trump uses your brain against you. He keeps repeating the same thing over and over, and every time he repeats it, it gets strengthened in your brain."[18] By the time Trump ran for president, the neural pathways linking his name to concepts like "success," "wealth," and "winning" had been so deeply established in millions of American minds that contrary evidence simply couldn't compete.

The Party That Knew and Followed Anyway

What's perhaps most revealing about Trump's rise to the presidency is that Republican insiders weren't fooled by his schtick. Unlike many ordinary voters who knew Trump only through *The Apprentice* and his carefully cultivated media image, GOP operatives and donors had seen the bankruptcies, the failed ventures, the lawsuits, and the erratic behavior right in front of them in real time.

"How do you abandon deeply held beliefs about character, personal responsibility, foreign policy, and the national debt in a matter of months?" asked Stuart Stevens, a veteran Republican strategist who had worked on multiple presidential campaigns. "You don't. The obvious answer is those beliefs weren't deeply held."[19]

Republican senators like Lindsey Graham called Trump a "kook," "crazy," and "unfit for office" during the 2016 primaries. Ted Cruz called him a "pathological liar." Marco Rubio mocked the size of his hands and questioned his business acumen.[20]

And yet, when it became clear that Trump had captured the Republican base through his performative aggression and racist dog whistles, the party's resistance collapsed with stunning speed. Once-fierce critics became sycophantic supporters. Principles that had defined conservatism for generations—free trade, fiscal responsibility, personal character, respect for the law, strong alliances—were abandoned overnight.

Why? Because Trump excited the base. He drew attention. He could dominate a news cycle without spending a dime. And, most importantly, he could win. For a party increasingly focused on power over principle, that was enough.

Mitch McConnell got judges. Paul Ryan got tax cuts. Evangelical leaders got Supreme Court justices who would overturn *Roe v. Wade*.

The bargain these Republican leaders made was cynical but straightforward: they would tolerate Trump's corruption, his cruelty, his attacks on the norms and standards that had been respected by presidents since George Washington, and his Russian entanglements in exchange for policy wins they couldn't achieve through democratic means. They pretended to believe the mask was real, knowing full well it wasn't, because the mask was useful to them and their donors.

It was Roy Cohn's final lesson—utility above truth in all cases—applied to governance itself.

They didn't get a president who embodied conservative principles or Christian values. They got a con man in chief. And they handed him the keys to our republic.

Why It Matters

Donald Trump didn't rise to power in spite of his failures; he rose because of how well he disguised them. He didn't build an empire. He built a mask. And when that mask stepped into politics, neither our media nor many of our voters asked what was behind it. They asked, instead, the horse-race question of whether or not it could win.

This is how democracies are gutted from within—not just through violence, but through illusion. Through celebrity. Through spectacle. Through the elevation of brand over truth. When perception matters more than reality, when performance trumps competence, when the simulation of strength is more compelling than actual leadership, the conditions are ripe for democratic collapse.

Trump's presidency would bring these assaults on decency to their logical conclusion. The same man who had pretended his way to business fame would now pretend his way through governance. The same tactics that allowed him to survive business failures would get him through political crises. The same indifference to truth that characterized his business career would now shape America's relationship with reality itself.

The mask of success that Trump had spent decades constructing would become the face of America to the world. And behind it, just as in his businesses, lay impending disaster—a pandemic response bungled, alliances fractured, democratic norms shattered, and ultimately, an insurrection incited.

Trump's mask is still on. But the damage it hides is all around us.

PART II

The System That Built Trump

The Beginning: The Machine That Eats Democracy

The liberty of a democracy is not safe if the people tolerated the growth of private power to a point where it becomes stronger than the democratic state itself. That in its essence is fascism: ownership of government by an individual, by a group, or any controlling private power. —Franklin D. Roosevelt, 1938 message to Congress

As Louise and I watched Trump descend that golden escalator in 2015, we felt what millions of Americans did: disbelief, followed by dismissal. Surely this reality TV showman, this serial bankrupt, this carnival barker would quickly fade. Yet as the years passed and my radio listeners increasingly reflected his worldview back to me, I confronted a haunting truth: Donald Trump didn't happen by accident.

He wasn't, as so many have suggested (particularly Democrats) just some political anomaly or a weird, media-driven glitch in American democracy. He was, instead, the inevitable product of political structures meticulously constructed by morbidly rich ideologues and the fossil fuel industry over decades; all systems designed to concentrate power in the executive branch, weaponize the historic grievances that have haunted American politics for three centuries, and systematically dismantle the democratic guardrails that, up until now, have kept us a free nation.

In Part I, we examined the making of the man: his father's cruelty, Roy Cohn's tutelage, and his carefully constructed façade of success. Now we must confront something far more disturbing: the billionaire- and corporate-funded "machinery" that made him possible.

The chapters ahead expose this anti-democratic infrastructure, built brick by brick, dollar by dollar, lie by lie over more than a half-century. We'll trace how the Republican Party transformed from Lincoln's vision of an egalitarian, democratic nation into a grievance-fueled vehicle for authoritarianism. We'll confront the dark money trail of billionaires who bought and paid for policy while helping encourage (particularly those who run media and social media outfits) populist rage.

We'll document how seizing control of our political systems by exploiting *Citizens United* and other corrupt Supreme Court decisions became a profit and power center for the unscrupulous, damaging large parts of the American middle class as they produced outsized dividends for shareholders. And we'll map the industrialization of lying, where truth itself became optional in service to power.

These aren't isolated phenomena. They form an interconnected system that not only enabled Trump but will outlast him. That's what makes this story so urgent. When we focus exclusively on the man, we miss the machinery that elevated him—a system still operating in communities across America—where legitimate economic suffering is weaponized to serve interests directly opposed to those experiencing the pain.

I've spent decades talking with Americans from all walks of life, from factory workers in Michigan (where Louise and I grew up) to farmers in Iowa to seniors in Florida. What strikes me is how many good people have been systematically lied to about the true causes of their hardship. The blueprint for American autocracy was refined over decades by those who found democracy too constraining for their ambitions. Understanding this blueprint is the first step toward dismantling it.

Because Republicans starting with the Reagan administration embraced the corrupt *Buckley, Bellotti,* and *Citizens United* decisions so aggressively, embracing and soliciting money from the morbidly rich, the

path ahead has the potential to be far darker than most Americans realize. But illuminating the machinery of democratic destruction is the necessary precondition to rebuilding what's been destroyed or weakened by
these greedy individuals. Because this isn't just about stopping Trump:
it's about exposing and then building public support for dismantling
the system that made him inevitable.

CHAPTER 4

The Party That Sold Itself Out

I hope we shall crush in its birth the aristocracy of our moneyed . . . corporations, which dare already to challenge our government to a trial of strength and bid defiance to the laws of our country. —Thomas Jefferson

IT WAS OCTOBER 10, 2016, AND THE WORLD WATCHED AS THE LAST CRED-ible, integrity-bound Republicans surrendered.

Just three days earlier, the infamous *Access Hollywood* tape had played on TVs worldwide. Donald Trump bragged about grabbing women "by the pussy," claiming that "when you're a star, they let you do it." The footage triggered a political firestorm. House Speaker Paul Ryan distanced himself, canceling a planned appearance with Trump. Senator John McCain withdrew his endorsement entirely. Utah Congressman Jason Chaffetz declared he could no longer support Trump while looking his fifteen-year-old daughter in the eye.

Louise and I watched the debate that followed on CNN. Trump stepped onstage in St. Louis, glowering. Rather than apologizing, he dismissed the comments as "locker room talk," deflected, and attacked Hillary Clinton's husband. He even threatened to imprison Clinton if elected: "You'd be in jail," he snarled. Throughout the evening, he physically stalked Clinton around the stage like a predator.[1]

The audience saw not a man apologizing, but dominating. That night, something remarkable happened. Instead of collapsing, Trump's poll numbers improved. The white "Christian" male-dominated Republican base, initially rattled, rapidly reconsolidated. Republican men didn't care what he'd said. They liked how he made them feel: powerful, angry, unrepentant.

By morning, Republicans crawled back into line. Chaffetz, less than seventy-two hours after declaring Trump immoral, tweeted: "I'm voting for Trump. HRC is that bad." Senator Deb Fischer of Nebraska, after calling on Trump to step aside, reversed herself: "I plan to vote for Mr. Trump," as if nothing had happened.[2]

A line had been crossed, but it didn't matter. Because Trump was winning. And the Republican Party had decided that winning was the only principle worth preserving.

This wasn't a hostile takeover of the GOP. This was its final form. That night didn't break the party; it revealed its post–Reagan Revolution's true character.

To understand how the Grand Old Party of Lincoln and Eisenhower became the grievance-fueled vehicle for Trump's authoritarian ambitions, we must trace its evolution over decades. Trump didn't create the modern Republican Party; he merely exploited and stripped away the last pretenses from a transformation decades in the making.

The Long Descent into Trumpism

Donald Trump didn't invent Republican cruelty, racial resentment, or truth denial. He inherited it. He perfected it.

The party that once claimed to be Lincoln's heir—founded to oppose slavery's expansion, that pushed for Reconstruction, that under Teddy Roosevelt championed conservation, the estate tax, and checked corporate power—had already

- Embraced the Southern Strategy, deliberately courting white racial resentment

- Turned dog whistles into bullhorns in its rhetoric about crime, welfare, and immigration

- Married billionaire donors with evangelical Christians in an unholy alliance of plutocracy and theocracy

- Transformed media from a source of shared facts into a propaganda machine

Trump simply lit the match that ignited this volatile mixture. But the kindling had been carefully stacked over decades with billions of dollars.

Nixon's Southern Strategy: The Blueprint of Betrayal

The modern Republican Party's transformation began with Richard Nixon and the 1968 election. America was in turmoil: the civil rights movement challenged long-standing racial hierarchies, the Vietnam War created generational conflict, and the assassinations of Martin Luther King Jr. and Robert Kennedy traumatized the nation.

As I detailed in *The Hidden History of the Supreme Court and the Betrayal of America*, we now know that President Johnson and Vice President Humphrey had worked out a peace deal with the Vietnamese by late summer 1968. Nixon, through an agent, reached out to the South Vietnamese and offered them support if they'd refuse to sign the deal, provoking Johnson to call Senator Everett Dirksen and complain that "this is treason." (Dirksen answered, "I know.") As a result, another million Vietnamese and over twenty thousand American GIs died during Nixon's presidency.[3]

But that was just the prelude to what would follow. Instead of appealing to America's better angels, Nixon saw opportunity in exploiting our historic demons. As Bill Moyers told me over dinner at Norman and Lyn Lear's home some years ago, when Democrats under Lyndon Johnson passed the Civil Rights Act of 1964 and the Voting Rights Act of 1965, they knew they were sacrificing their once-solid grip on the South. Johnson, Moyers said, proclaimed after signing the Civil Rights Act words to the effect of, "We have lost the South for a generation."[4]

Nixon saw these disaffected white Southern voters as key to a new Republican majority. Thus was born the GOP's "Southern Strategy," a deliberate effort to appeal to white racial anxieties without explicitly racist language.

Nixon's political strategist Kevin Phillips was remarkably candid in a 1970 *New York Times* article: "From now on, the Republicans are never going to get more than 10 to 20 percent of the Negro vote and they don't need any more than that. . . . The more Negroes who register as Democrats in the South, the sooner the Negrophobe whites will quit the Democrats and become Republicans. That's where the votes are."[5]

Instead of saying the N-word, Republicans began using coded phrases like "law and order," "states' rights," and "forced busing." As strategist Lee Atwater would later admit in a candid 1981 interview: "You start out in 1954 by saying, 'N-word, N-word, N-word.' By 1968, you can't say 'N-word'—that hurts you. So you say stuff like forced busing, states' rights. . . . You're getting so abstract. 'We want to cut this,' is much more abstract than even the busing thing, and a hell of a lot more abstract than 'N-word.'"[6]

This strategy paid massive dividends. In the 1968 election, Nixon won five Southern states that had been Democratic strongholds for generations. In 1972, he swept every Southern state, cynically redrawing the map of American politics along racial lines.[7]

Reagan: The Smile on the Guillotine

If Nixon provided the blueprint for the Republican Party's racial strategy, Ronald Reagan perfected its execution. With his Hollywood charm, Reagan could deliver messages with a smile that would have sounded sinister from Nixon.

On August 3, 1980, Reagan chose to launch his general election campaign in Philadelphia, Mississippi, where three civil rights workers had been murdered by the Ku Klux Klan in 1964. Standing near the site of this infamous racial crime (later made into the movie *Mississippi Burning*), Reagan declared: "I believe in states' rights."[8] Nobody in the all-white audience misunderstood his meaning; with Reagan, the GOP had perfected the art of the racial dog whistle.

Once in office, Reagan deployed cultural scapegoats with surgical precision. He invented the myth of the "welfare queen," supposedly a Chicago woman who "has 80 names, 30 addresses, 12 Social Security cards and is collecting veteran's benefits on four non-existing deceased husbands." Though never explicitly identifying her as Black, the racial subtext was abundantly clear.[9]

Reagan gave America a powerful myth: that minorities, "welfare cheats," and "liberal elites" were the problem, not billionaires and corporations rigging the economy. He wrapped regressive economics in racial, gender, and cultural resentment, teaching Republicans that plutocracy could win elections if sufficiently disguised.

Trump would later repeat this formula almost verbatim, just louder, cruder, and without Reagan's disciplined delivery. The difference was not one of kind, but of degree.[10]

The Parasitic Takeover

In my analysis, the relationship between Republican leaders and their party wasn't just political: it was parasitic. Each successive Republican figure injected their ideological "eggs" into the party's body politic. Nixon implanted the first "eggs" of racism with his "silent majority" rhetoric and "war on drugs," designed to disrupt civil rights movements. Reagan then incubated these tendencies with his "welfare queen" comments.

What makes Trump's takeover remarkable isn't that he introduced something entirely new, but that he fully consumed a host corrupted over decades, first by Nixon's scandals, then by Reagan's policies undermining middle-class security, and finally by Bush and Cheney's tax cuts and disastrous wars. Like the cordyceps fungus that infects ants and controls their behavior, Trump didn't just lead the GOP; he seized control of its brain, redirecting its behavior while feeding on its institutional body.[11]

Gingrich and the Media Machine: The Death of Truth

If Reagan provided the ideological framework, Newt Gingrich and Roger Ailes revolutionized the tactical approach, turning American politics from an adversarial but functional system into a zero-sum blood sport, the perfect foundation for Trump.

Gingrich became Speaker of the House in January 1995 following an explosion of billionaire money and right-wing media characterizing President Clinton's first two years as corrupt and socialist. He explicitly rejected the traditional view that politicians should work across the aisle for the common good. Instead, he preached that politics should be played like warfare, with enemies and few rules of engagement.

Gingrich published a 1990 memo titled "Language: A Key Mechanism of Control," instructing Republican candidates to refer to Democrats with words like "traitors," "pathetic," "sick," "corrupt," and "anti-flag." The memo, distributed through his GOPAC organization, included lists of negative "contrasting words" to be used about Democrats and "opti-mistic positive governing words" for Republicans. It wasn't about policy disagreements but using the media to demonize Democrats to justify refusing to cooperate.[12]

Simultaneously, in October 1996, Rupert Murdoch and Roger Ailes launched *Fox News*, transforming not just the media landscape but the American mind itself. Fox presented itself as a corrective to "liberal bias." Its slogan, "Fair and Balanced," implied that other news sources were unfair. But from the beginning, Fox was designed not to inform but to influence, creating a parallel information ecosystem where conservative narratives were presented as fact.[13]

By 2011, a Fairleigh Dickinson University study found that *Fox News* viewers were less informed about current events than people who watched no news at all.[14] Fox wasn't adding information; it was replacing it with alternative narratives.

The combination was lethal for democracy and laid the foundation for today's MAGA GOP. Gingrich preached that compromise was weak-ness and government itself was the enemy. *Fox News* gave Republicans a nationwide bullhorn. Together, they created an environment where facts became optional, conspiracy theories flourished, and loyalty to party leadership superseded commitment to America herself.[15]

As Norm Ornstein of the American Enterprise Institute observed, the Republican Party had become "an insurgent outlier, ideologically extreme; contemptuous of the inherited social and economic policy regime; scornful of compromise; unpersuaded by conventional under-standing of facts, evidence, and science; and dismissive of the legitimacy of its political opposition."[16]

The Tea Party: Astroturf Insurrection

On inauguration day, January 20, 2009, as Louise and I danced in Union Station with America's first Black president and his wife, a group of Repub-lican leaders gathered at the Caucus Room restaurant next door to what was then our Washington apartment to plot Obama's destruction. Their plan, as reported by journalist Robert Draper, was simple: "Show united and unyielding opposition to the president's economic policies. . . . Win the spear point of the House in 2010. Jab Obama relentlessly in 2011. Win the White House and the Senate in 2012."[17]

This wasn't about policy disagreements. It was, in Senator Mitch McConnell's infamous words, about ensuring that "the single most important thing we want to achieve is for President Obama to be a one-term president."[18]

After this meeting, Republicans could have collaborated with Obama on addressing the worst economic crisis since the Great Depression. Instead, they declared total war, voting unanimously against the American Recovery and Reinvestment Act despite the economy losing 800,000 jobs monthly.

But formal Republican opposition wasn't enough. The party needed a movement: something appearing grassroots but directed from above. Enter the Tea Party.

Ostensibly sparked by CNBC commentator Rick Santelli's February 2009 rant against mortgage relief, the Tea Party presented itself as a spontaneous uprising of citizens concerned about government spending and debt.

In reality, it was "astroturf": fake grassroots. Behind the seemingly organic protests were well-funded conservative organizations like Americans for Prosperity and FreedomWorks, backed by fossil fuel billionaires like the Kochs. These groups provided money, messaging, transportation, coordination with right-wing media, and organizational infrastructure for Tea Party rallies.[19] Investigative reporting documented how the Koch brothers' network poured millions into creating and sustaining this seemingly spontaneous "movement."[20]

What made the Tea Party potent wasn't just its corporate backing but its racial subtext. Protesters carried signs showing Obama as a witch doctor with a bone through his nose. They questioned his citizenship, his religion, his very Americanness. Their rallying cry—"We want our country back"—had a clear implication: they wanted an all-white power structure to return.

A 2010 University of Washington study by Professor Christopher Parker found that 73 percent of Tea Party supporters agreed that "Irish, Italians, Jewish, and many other minorities overcame prejudice and worked their way up. Blacks should do the same without special favors."[21] Further research demonstrated that racial resentment was a stronger predictor of Tea Party support than concerns about government spending.[22]

This radicalized base—trained to hate compromise and question democratic governance—was perfectly primed for a wannabe autocrat like Trump. When he began his campaign questioning Obama's American birth, he was speaking directly to a Tea Party audience explicitly cultivated for this message.

The GOP Purge: From Moderates to Mini-Trumps

From 2010 onward, the Republican Party underwent a purge that would have impressed Stalin. Moderate Republicans—willing to occasionally reach across the aisle, believing in governance rather than obstruction— were systematically eliminated.

The mechanisms were numerous:

- Primary challenges against any Republican failing to demonstrate sufficient ideological purity. Congressman Bob Inglis of South Carolina, with a 93 percent lifetime rating from the American Conservative Union, lost his primary in 2010 after acknowledging climate change. Senator Richard Lugar of Indiana, a six-term senator with impeccable conservative credentials, was defeated in 2012 for occasionally working with Democrats.[23]

- Gerrymandered districts where the only electoral threat came from the right. After the 2010 census, Republican state legislatures redrew congressional maps to create safe districts where moderation was political suicide.[24]

- Purity tests on issues from guns to abortion to taxes. Groups like the Club for Growth, Americans for Tax Reform, and the National Rifle Association established rigid litmus tests enforced through scorecards and primary challenge threats.[25]

The result was a dramatic rightward shift. Analysis by the Lugar Center showed that bipartisanship in Congress collapsed after 2010— coinciding with the Citizens United decision that gave billionaires and corporations the legal ability to buy politicians—with Republicans especially unwilling to cross party lines.[26]

By 2015, the party had become a machine rewarding cruelty, extremism, and blind loyalty over the good of the country or policy knowledge. It didn't matter that Trump mocked POWs like John McCain ("I like people who weren't captured") or bragged about sexual assault. He could "own the libs," the ultimate virtue in the new Republican Party.

Why They All Fell in Line or Were Purged

When Trump won the GOP's nomination in 2016, Republican power brokers faced a choice:

- Reject a demagogue with no governmental experience or commitment to democratic norms, or

- Embrace him and get everything they'd dreamed of: tax cuts for the rich, deregulation, conservative judges, and a president who would sign whatever legislation they put before him.

They chose power. Trump gave them:

- Tax cuts: The 2017 Tax Cuts and Jobs Act delivered the largest corporate tax cut in American history, slashing the top personal rate from 39.6 percent to 37 percent and the corporate rate from 35 percent to 21 percent. Analysis found the cuts were a massive boon to corporations and the richest Americans, with minimal benefits for workers despite GOP trickle-down claims.[27]

- Right-wing judges: Trump appointed three Supreme Court justices—Gorsuch, Kavanaugh, and Barrett—cementing a 6–3 conservative majority. Beyond that, he appointed 234 federal judges—nearly 30 percent of the entire federal judiciary—most vetted by the Federalist Society to advance conservative and corporate interests.[28]

- A fanatical base: Trump energized the Republican base like no candidate since Reagan, bringing in previously disengaged voters, particularly whites without college degrees who responded to his racial appeals and anti-elite messaging (ironic coming from a college-educated billionaire born to wealth).[29]

In exchange, Republicans gave Trump absolute loyalty. They defended his worst excesses, excused his attacks on democratic norms, and turned a blind eye to corruption that would have ended any other presidency.

This wasn't fear: it was calculation. A Faustian bargain made with clear understanding of the trade-offs. Republican leaders decided that power—even temporary power wielded by someone they privately considered unfit—was worth sacrificing their stated principles, constitutional duties, and self-respect.

Senator Lindsey Graham's transformation encapsulates this bargain. In 2015, Graham called Trump "a race-baiting, xenophobic, religious bigot" who was "not fit to be president." By 2019, he had become one of Trump's most ardent defenders, telling reporters, "To every Republican: If you don't stand behind this president, we're not going to stand behind you."[30]

The shift wasn't just hypocritical: it was the logical endpoint of a party that had decided winning was its only principle.

Why It Matters

Donald Trump didn't destroy the Republican Party. He completed it. He brought it full circle:

- From Lincoln, the Great Emancipator, to Lee Atwater's racial coding

- From Eisenhower, who warned about the military-industrial complex, to a party captured by corporate interests

- From Teddy Roosevelt, the trust-buster, to a party celebrating monopolies

- From Reagan's "shining city on a hill" to "American carnage"

- And from dog whistles to bullhorns in its appeals to white grievance

The GOP spent decades feeding the beast of white resentment, oligarchic power, and media manipulation. Trump put a new face on it and branded it with his name in gold letters.

He was not the disease. He was the final symptom; the fever making the infection impossible to ignore.

As we discovered after Trump's 2020 defeat, when Republicans embraced his Big Lie about election fraud and facilitated an attempted coup, the party had completed its transformation from a traditional conservative organization into something far more dangerous: a personality cult willing to sacrifice the peaceful transfer of power—the bedrock of democratic governance—to maintain its grip on power.[31]

And now, in his second term, we're seeing constraints on his worst impulses tossed aside as he surrounds himself with loyal sycophants, defies courts, targets enemies, corrupts government agencies, and sucks up to Vladimir Putin in a way that would have horrified even Nixon, Reagan, or both Bushes.

The response to the *Access Hollywood* tape moment of October 2016 wasn't just Republican hypocrisy. It was a preview of the moral and constitutional abdication to come, when standing up for any principle became secondary to standing with their leader, no matter where he led them.

Even into insurrection. Even into anti-American lawlessness. Even into the abyss.

CHAPTER 5

Powered by Plutocrats

There is absolutely nothing to be said for government by a plutocracy, for government by men very powerful in certain lines and gifted with "the money touch," but with ideals which in their essence are merely those of so many glorified pawnbrokers.
—Theodore Roosevelt, 1913 letter to Sir Edward Grey

MAKE NO MISTAKE: TRUMP WASN'T PRESIDENT BECAUSE OF HIS POLICIES, his qualifications, or even primarily because of his base. He was president because America's wealthiest class funded his rise, protected his power, and enabled his worst instincts, at least so long as he delivered the goods.

Reporter Kayla Kitson documents, for example, how the Koch brothers invested roughly $40 million in promoting the 2017 Trump tax cut for billionaires and reaped a $500 million-a-year tax cut for themselves and over a billion dollars for their company. She notes, "The propaganda for the Republican Tax Act portrays it as good for investment. It's hard to find an investment in the real economy that paid off as handsomely as the Koch brothers' political spending."[1]

The billionaires funding Trump generally weren't concerned with his character, his corruption, or his contempt for constitutional governance. They saw in him a uniquely useful tool, a president with no fixed principles beyond self-enrichment, willing to hand over the mechanics of government to those who had paid for his ascent, as we see now with his implementation of Project 2025.

And deliver he did. The tax legislation that prompted Kochs' windfall during his first term provided the largest corporate tax cut in American history, slashing rates from 35 percent to 21 percent permanently, while offering temporary crumbs to the middle class that would quickly expire. For the ultra-wealthy and corporations, it was the fulfillment of decades-long dreams.[2]

That wasn't policy; it was plunder. An upward wealth transfer of unprecedented scale was disguised—as Reagan and Bush had done before him, driving our nation's debt above $34 trillion—as economic stimulus.

And this grand theft happened right in front of the American people, who were too distracted by the daily spectacle of Trump's outrages to notice that it was as if the Treasury was being looted by billionaires in broad daylight.

To understand how America's democracy became vulnerable to such brazen capture—how Lincoln's "government of the people, by the people, and for the people" could be so thoroughly transformed into a vehicle for plutocratic enrichment—you must first understand not just Trump himself but the sophisticated system that elevated him to power, directed his administration's actions, and profited from the chaos he created.

Citizens United: The Corporate Coup by a Corrupt Supreme Court

The groundwork for the GOP's plutocratic takeover of American politics was laid on January 21, 2010, when the Supreme Court issued a ruling that fundamentally transformed American politics. In *Citizens United v. Federal Election Commission*, the court's 5–4 Republican majority struck down key provisions of campaign finance laws dating all the way back to the late nineteenth century, ruling that corporations and outside groups could spend functionally unlimited sums on elections through the Super PACs the decision invented.

Justice Anthony Kennedy, writing for the majority, made the extraordinary claim that "independent expenditures, including those made by corporations, do not give rise to corruption or the appearance of corruption."[3] This statement would soon be revealed as one of the most naïve or cynical pronouncements in Supreme Court history.

This wasn't merely a legal technicality: it was the culmination of a century-long corporate campaign to claim the Constitutional rights of persons while avoiding the responsibilities of citizenship. As I've documented extensively in my books *Unequal Protection* and *The Hidden*

History of the Supreme Court and the Betrayal of America, corporations had methodically pursued personhood since the 1886 Santa Clara County Supreme Court case, gradually acquiring First Amendment protections, Fourth Amendment rights against unreasonable searches, Fifth Amendment protections against self-incrimination, and Fourteenth Amendment equal protection claims.

Citizens United represented their ultimate victory, handing them the power to flood our democratic processes with unlimited cash while remaining legally obligated solely to maximize shareholder returns. American democracy was being transformed into what Franklin Roosevelt once called "economic royalism," aka rule by the economic elite rather than we the people.

Unlike the First Gilded Age, when robber barons like J. P. Morgan and John D. Rockefeller primarily purchased individual politicians, this Second Gilded Age enabled the wholesale capture of our political system itself. The American experiment in self-governance—unique in its founding premise that all political power originates from the people themselves—was being fundamentally rewired to ensure that political power originated from those holding or controlling great wealth. And Trump, himself a product of inherited wealth with an instinctive deference to monied interests despite his populist rhetoric, was the perfect vehicle for this transformation.

The practical effects were immediate and profound. Political spending by outside groups exploded, jumping from $750 million in the 2008 presidential election to over $4.5 billion in 2016.[4] But more significant than the amount was the source: just 150 billionaire families put up more than 60 percent of all Super PAC money raised in the years following Citizens United.[5]

It was no longer one person, one vote. It was one billionaire, one megaphone, with the volume turned up to deafening levels.

Into this system stepped the new American oligarchs, whose names would become synonymous with the corruption of American democracy: the Koch brothers, Charles and David, whose combined fortune from their fossil fuel and industrial conglomerate exceeded $100 billion, built a political machine larger than the Republican National Committee itself, with tentacles extending into every aspect of conservative politics.

Robert Mercer, a reclusive hedge fund billionaire whose algorithmic trading firm, Renaissance Technologies, generated billions through high-frequency trading while reportedly trying to avoid billions in taxes through complex financial engineering.[6]

Sheldon Adelson, the casino magnate who once suggested dropping a nuclear bomb on Iran as a negotiating tactic, poured more than $100 million into Trump's presidential campaigns.[7]

These men and their billionaire colleagues didn't, in my opinion, want democracy; they wanted control. Control over a government that might otherwise regulate their industries, tax their enormous wealth, or hold them accountable for environmental and social damage their businesses caused.

Citizens United gave them the tools to seize that control. And in Donald Trump, they found the perfect front man for their operation.

The Trump-Mercer Alliance

By August 2016, just four critical months short of that year's election, Donald Trump's presidential campaign was floundering. After a disastrous convention peppered with an absurd assortment of weirdos and freaks, along with weeks of self-inflicted wounds, he was trailing Hillary Clinton in every swing state.

His campaign organization—run by Putin's oligarchs' man Paul Manafort who'd earlier helped Putin take control of Ukraine's politics— was skeletal, and most political observers agreed that it lacked the basic infrastructure needed to win. Traditional Republican donors were keeping their distance as rumors of Russian influence swirled, and President Hillary seemed a fait accompli. The nation's political observers were preparing to write the obituary for an unconventional (and deeply racist) campaign that had captured attention but failed to build the type of traditional boots-on-the-ground machinery necessary to win.[8]

Then, in August, everything changed. Trump welcomed two oligarchs who would transform his campaign and ultimately the country: Robert Mercer and his daughter Rebekah.

Few Americans knew who the Mercers were. Robert, a former IBM computer scientist turned hedge fund billionaire, was so reclusive that many of his own employees had never heard him speak. Rebekah, his politically ambitious daughter, operated largely behind the scenes, leveraging her father's fortune to gain influence in conservative politics.

As reporter Jane Mayer wrote, "Last summer, Bannon and some other activists whom the Mercers have supported—including David Bossie, who initiated the Citizens United lawsuit—came together to rescue Trump's wobbly campaign. Sam Nunberg, an early Trump adviser who watched Mercer's group take over, said, 'Mercer was smart. He invested in the right people.'"

That August meeting appears to have resulted in an immediate campaign shakeup. Out went campaign chairman Paul Manafort. In came two Mercer loyalists: Steve Bannon, the executive chairman of Breitbart News (which the Mercers had funded with $10 million), and Kellyanne Conway, who had previously run a Mercer-backed Super PAC for Ted Cruz.[9]

This wasn't just a change in personnel. It was a complete takeover of the Trump campaign by the Mercer political machine. With this takeover came the resources that would prove decisive: Cambridge Analytica, a data firm in which the Mercers were principal investors, had harvested personal data from more than 50 million Facebook users without their consent. This treasure trove of psychological profiles allowed the Trump campaign to micro-target voters with messages precisely calibrated to their fears, resentments, and personal vulnerabilities.[10]

Breitbart News was the far-right website that had become a key platform for white nationalism and conspiracy theories. Under Bannon's leadership and with Mercer funding, Breitbart had grown from an obscure blog to a powerful media force driving the Republican Party rightward.

The Mercers apparently didn't back Trump because they personally admired him or thought he would make a good president. Rebekah Mercer had initially supported Ted Cruz, considering Trump a showman lacking serious conservative credentials.

Instead, they appear to have backed him because they recognized in him a vessel; someone whose personal characteristics (his celebrity status, shamelessness, and instinctive understanding of mass psychology) made him uniquely positioned to advance their ideological agenda. That agenda included dismantling the administrative state, slashing taxes on the wealthy, eliminating environmental regulations, and transforming the judiciary through far-right appointments.

"The Mercers laid the groundwork for the Trump revolution," Steve Bannon would later acknowledge. "Irrefutably, when you look at donors during the past four years, they have had the single biggest impact of anybody, including the Kochs."[11]

The alliance proved remarkably successful. Within weeks, Trump's poll numbers rebounded. His messaging became more disciplined (if no less extreme). The campaign's digital operation began outperforming Clinton's vaunted data team. And on election night, against all traditional polling predictions, Trump secured narrow victories in key swing states.

The Mercers had made their bet. And it was about to pay off spectacularly.

The Tax Cuts and the GOP's Greatest Heist

I've been writing about economic policy in America for over thirty years, and I've never seen a more brazen transfer of wealth from the working class to the morbidly rich than the Tax Cuts and Jobs Act of 2017.

On December 22, 2017, Donald Trump signed this legislation into law; it was the most significant achievement of his first-term presidency (outside of letting 400,000 Americans die unnecessarily of COVID). Standing in the Oval Office, surrounded by gleeful Republican lawmakers with sugarplums of giant campaign donations dancing in their eyes, Trump boasted that the bill would bring "tremendous relief for the middle class and small businesses."[12]

It was a claim that bore little relation to reality. Though marketed as middle-class tax relief, the legislation was, in fact, a $1.9 trillion giveaway to corporations and the ultra-wealthy, precisely the outcome that Trump's billionaire backers had been seeking.

The centerpiece was a permanent reduction in the corporate tax rate from 35 percent to 21 percent, a change that delivered hundreds of billions to America's largest companies. While workers were promised higher wages through trickle-down effects, corporations primarily used their windfall for stock buybacks, a practice Reagan legalized that enriches shareholders and executives while doing nothing for employees or long-term investment.

In the first year after the tax cut, US corporations announced over $1 trillion in stock buybacks, setting an all-time record.[13] Meanwhile, the "wage boom" promised to workers failed to materialize, just as when Reagan and Bush had made similar promises after their massive tax cuts. A Congressional Research Service analysis found "no indication of a surge in wages" attributable to the tax cuts.[14]

Beyond the corporate rate reduction, the bill contained provisions carefully tailored to benefit the wealthiest Americans:

- A 20 percent deduction for "pass-through" business income, which particularly benefited real estate developers (including Trump himself) and wealthy business owners who structure their income through LLCs rather than as traditional wage income

- Gutting of the estate tax by doubling the exemption to $22 million for married couples, ensuring that only the wealthiest 0.1 percent of estates would face the tax

The benefits flowed directly to those who had funded Trump's rise. Charles Koch estimated the bill would save his empire $1.4 billion annually. Sheldon Adelson's Las Vegas Sands Corporation saw its effective tax rate drop from 34 percent to 20.6 percent. The Mercers' Renaissance Technologies benefited enormously from both corporate rate reductions and the preferential treatment of pass-through income.

Even Trump himself stood to gain tens of millions through the real estate provisions and pass-through deductions, though we can't know the exact amount since he broke with decades of presidential precedent by refusing to release his tax returns.

"Our [wealthy/corporate] donors are basically saying, 'Get it done or don't ever call me again,'" Republican Congressman Chris Collins admitted, referring to the tax bill.[15]

This wasn't policy in any traditional sense. It wasn't designed to address national challenges, strengthen the economy's foundations, or improve the lives of most Americans. It was plunder, pure and simple: a massive upward redistribution of wealth to the GOP's donor class that had purchased the presidency with the blessing of five corrupt Republicans on the Supreme Court.

And the politicians who passed it? They were rewarded handsomely with campaign cash, dark money advertising support, and the promise of lucrative post-legislative lobbying jobs. In the three months after the tax bill passed, the Koch network announced plans to spend $20 million promoting the legislation and $400 million on the 2018 midterm elections to protect the lawmakers who had voted for it.[16]

The cycle was now complete: billionaires funded politicians who passed laws benefiting billionaires who then provided more funding to those same politicians. Democracy as perpetual motion machine, if your definition of democracy is government of, by, and exclusively for the wealthiest Americans.

The Distraction Presidency

While most Americans focused on Trump's latest tweets, his attacks on celebrities, his feuds with NFL players kneeling during the national anthem, or his dark warnings about immigrant caravans, his billionaire backers were quietly reshaping the country's institutional architecture in ways that would long outlast his presidency.

Trump was the perfect vehicle for this strategy. His ability to dominate media attention—to ensure that every news cycle revolved around his latest outrage—created the ideal cover for the systematic dismantling of regulatory protections and installation of corporate allies throughout government.

Behind this all-consuming spectacle, the real work of the plutocratic agenda proceeded:

Judicial appointments: The Federalist Society, heavily funded by the Koch network, the Mercers, and other right-wing billionaires, effectively outsourced the selection of federal judges to Trump. Leonard Leo, the society's cochairman, reportedly developed the list of Supreme Court candidates from which Trump selected Neil Gorsuch, Brett Kavanaugh, and Amy Coney Barrett, cementing a 6–3 conservative majority likely to last for a generation.

Beyond the Supreme Court, as mentioned earlier, Trump appointed

234 federal judges—nearly 30 percent of the entire federal judiciary—many of them young, ideologically extreme, and handpicked by the Federalist Society to advance corporate interests and limit government regulatory power to protect consumers, the environment, and democracy itself.[17]

Environmental deregulation: Koch-funded pro-fossil fuel groups like the American Energy Alliance and the Competitive Enterprise Institute helped advise the administration in how to dismantle over one hundred environmental protections, including Obama-era regulations on clean water, methane emissions, and fuel efficiency. These changes handed billions in additional profits to fossil fuel companies while increasing cancer and climate change risks for the rest of us. Scott Pruitt, who had previously sued the EPA fourteen times, was appointed by Trump to head that same agency.[18]

Financial deregulation: Wall Street billionaires who'd backed Trump saw their agenda executed by weakening Elizabeth Warren's Consumer Financial Protection Bureau (CFPB), the gutting of banking regulations implemented after the 2008 financial crisis, and the appointment of industry allies up and down the government to key regulatory posts. In 2025, Trump and Musk tried to cripple or even shut down the CFPB and, as of this writing, it's before the courts.[19]

As with his second administration but without the preparation of Project 2025, Trump was the show throughout his first. The billionaires were the directors: setting the agenda, writing the script, and reaping the profits while the American public remained captivated by the daily drama, "The Trump Show," emanating from the White House.

Selling Out the Planet

Perhaps nowhere was the influence of plutocratic donors more evident—or more destructive—than in the Trump administration's environmental policies. On June 1, 2017, Trump announced that the United States would withdraw from the Paris Climate Agreement, fulfilling a campaign promise to his fossil fuel patrons and making America one of only four nations on Earth to reject this landmark accord to combat climate change.

Standing in the Rose Garden, Trump claimed he was putting "American workers first." The reality was that he was putting fossil fuel executives and their shareholders first, at the expense of not just workers but the habitability of our planet itself.

This decision didn't emerge from a thoughtful review of evidence or a careful weighing of national interests. It emerged directly from the fossil fuel industry's wish list, delivered to the White House through a network of industry-funded think tanks, lobbyists, and political donors.

In the weeks leading up to the announcement, Trump heard from a parade of fossil fuel advocates:

- The American Petroleum Institute, the oil and gas industry's main lobbying group, which had contributed millions to Republican campaigns

- Coal company executives like Robert Murray of Murray Energy, a major Trump donor who had provided the administration with an "action plan" calling for rollbacks of environmental regulations

- The Heritage Foundation, which received significant funding from oil companies and the Koch network and would largely produce Project 2025 for his second attempt at deconstructing the American government

These voices drowned out others within the administration who argued that withdrawal would damage US interests. Even Secretary of State Rex Tillerson, the former CEO of ExxonMobil, reportedly advised staying in the agreement.

But they couldn't compete with the donors. The Koch network alone had spent over $88 million funding climate change denial, according to a Drexel University study.[20] Now they were calling in their investment.

The Paris withdrawal was just the beginning. Over the next four years, the Trump administration would roll back Obama's Clean Power Plan, weaken fuel efficiency standards for automobiles, open previously protected public lands to drilling, eliminate regulations on methane leaks from oil and gas operations, and appoint former coal industry lobbyist Andrew Wheeler to lead the Environmental Protection Agency after Scott Pruitt resigned amid multiple ethics scandals.

Each of these decisions could be traced back to fossil fuel industry requests, often delivered through the same network of donors, think tanks, and lobbying groups that had funded Trump's rise to power.

The possibility of climate collapse wasn't a bug of the Trump presidency: it was a feature, an outcome of a system captured by fossil fuel interests willing to sacrifice the planet's future for short-term profits.

January 6: They Funded That Too

When a violent mob stormed the United States Capitol on January 6, 2021, attempting to overturn the results of the 2020 presidential election, many of America's corporate leaders and billionaire donors issued statements expressing shock and dismay. They condemned the violence, called for a peaceful transition of power, and presented themselves as defenders of democratic norms against extremism.

But this performative outrage couldn't obscure a fundamental reality: many of the same donors who had funded Trump's rise, who had tolerated his attacks on democratic norms, who had profited from his policies, had helped create the conditions that made the insurrection possible.

The connections were often direct: the Republican Attorneys General Association, funded by corporate donors, including Koch Industries, Altria, Comcast, and Walmart, had helped organize the January 6 "March to Save America" rally that preceded the Capitol riot. The group's fundraising arm, the Rule of Law Defense Fund, sent robocalls encouraging Trump supporters to come to Washington and "fight to protect the integrity of our elections."[21]

Major GOP donors including Home Depot cofounder Bernie Marcus, shipping magnate Richard Uihlein, and MyPillow CEO Mike Lindell bankrolled organizations and campaigns that spread the "Big Lie" about election fraud, creating the grievance that fueled the insurrection.[22] Charlie Kirk's Turning Point USA, heavily funded by Republican megadonors, boasted that it had sent "80+ buses of patriots to DC to fight for the president" on January 6.

Even after the violence, the donor class quickly returned to business as usual. A Reuters analysis found that most major corporations resumed political donations to Republican lawmakers who had voted against certifying the election results, after briefly pausing contributions in the immediate aftermath of the insurrection.[23]

The American oligarchy wasn't shocked by what happened on January 6. Many of them were right in the middle of the process of creating the conditions that made it possible. They had funded the politicians who spread the Big Lie, owned or sponsored the media outlets that amplified it, and helped the organizations that mobilized the mob.

Why would America's billionaire class tolerate, and in some cases actively support, an assault on democracy itself? Because Trump's chaos had served them well, distracting the public while they consolidated their power through deregulation, tax cuts, and judicial appointments. Because many of them had come to see democracy itself—with its potential for majority rule, progressive taxation, and regulation in the public interest—as an obstacle to their agenda rather than a system to be preserved.

Why It Matters

Trump was never the architect of the transformation of American governance during his first presidency. He was the wrecking ball funded by the architects: the billionaire class that had identified him as the perfect vehicle for their agenda of deregulation, tax cuts, and judicial capture.

Five corrupt Republicans on the Supreme Court, several famously the beneficiaries of billionaire largesse, created a system that allows billionaires to buy judges and elections, write policy, and silence opposition. This isn't democracy in, as Roosevelt would say, any meaningful sense of the word. It's oligarchy, as Jimmy Carter told me in 2010 when he said on my radio program: "[Citizens United] violates the essence of what made America a great country in its political system. Now it's just an oligarchy, with unlimited political bribery being the essence of getting the nominations for president or to elect the president. . . . So now we've just seen a complete subversion of our political system as a payoff to major contributors, who want and expect and sometimes get favors for themselves after the election's over."[24]

And Donald Trump—loud, crude, constantly demanding attention while lacking any coherent ideology beyond self-promotion—was the perfect pitchman for this oligarchic operation. He provided the spectacle, the outrage, the endless drama that kept Americans divided and distracted while the real work of plutocratic entrenchment proceeded behind the scenes.

His first term wasn't just a presidency: it was a heist. And now this same sophisticated operation to transfer wealth and power upward on an unprecedented scale, using cultural grievance and racial resentment as cover for economic plunder, has again been inflicted on us.

With all the focus on Trump's excesses, it's important to remember that the most dangerous threat to American democracy isn't a single authoritarian leader. He can be impeached or stopped by the courts or Congress, should they rise to the occasion.

Instead, it's the system that produces such leaders and keeps them from being challenged because members of their own party are terrified of millions of dollars being spent to politically destroy them if they stray. This system, in which unimaginable concentrations of wealth translate directly into unaccountable political power, in which elections are bought and policies are purchased, in which government of, by, and for the people has been replaced by government of, by, and for the donor class, is what keeps Trump in office and the crisis of democracy boiling.

Until we confront this system—until we recognize that the problem isn't just Trump but the machinery that created him—we will remain vulnerable to the damage he's doing right now, as well as the possibility of a future charismatic demagogue willing to serve as the battering ram for plutocratic power.

Because the billionaires are still there, still funding, still planning. And, like Fritz Thyssen in 1930s Germany, they've learned that investing in authoritarianism pays extraordinary dividends, at least over the short term. (Thyssen eventually had to flee for his life.)

CHAPTER 6

The Death of Democracy Is Profitable

We can have democracy in this country, or we can have great wealth concentrated in the hands of a few, but we can't have both. —Louis D. Brandeis, *Other People's Money*

J AKELIN CAAL MAQUIN WAS ONLY SEVEN YEARS OLD WHEN SHE DIED IN the custody of our government.

This little girl with bright brown eyes had journeyed thousands of miles from Guatemala's remote highlands with her father, Nery Caal. Unlike the immigrants constantly demonized by Trump, they followed the law, surrendering to Border Patrol agents at a legal port of entry in New Mexico and formally requesting asylum.

Already ill upon arrival, Jakelin's condition was ignored. When she began vomiting and having seizures during a bus transfer, there was no medical equipment to help her. By the time they reached a hospital in El Paso, her body temperature had peaked at 105.9 degrees. She died fewer than forty-eight hours after arriving in the United States from dehydration, shock, and liver failure.[1]

The Department of Homeland Security immediately deflected responsibility, claiming the family hadn't consumed food or water for days. Her father quickly exposed this lie through an attorney, stating they had adequate sustenance throughout their journey.[2]

No translator was present during intake. Forms were in English, a language neither spoke. The facility was overcrowded, understaffed, and with far from adequate medical care.

Trump's new system—designed to punish, not protect—functioned exactly as intended.

While Jakelin's story briefly made headlines, another story didn't: the one playing out on Wall Street in the weeks following her death. Stock prices for CoreCivic and GEO Group, two of America's largest private prison companies, rose steadily. These corporations made fortunes from contracts to manage ICE detention centers, contracts made possible by Trump's brutal immigration policies. Their business model depended on keeping migrants detained as long as possible at the lowest possible cost.[3]

This wasn't just tragic. It was profitable.

Throughout my decades as an entrepreneur—from starting The Electronics Joint in East Lansing when I was seventeen to my current radio program—I've never encountered businesspeople who deliberately set out to profit from human suffering. Yet here we are, in supposedly the most advanced democracy on Earth, watching a machinery of cruelty generating reliable returns for investors.

Jakelin's death wasn't an accident or the result of a "broken" system. It was the inevitable outcome of a system transformed to serve profits over people. The GOP's multidecade embrace of "public/private partnerships" outsourcing government functions to for-profit industry has produced a system where cruelty isn't a bug: it's a feature.

The Business of Cruelty

The defining feature of Trump's governance is transactional authoritarianism like in Hungary or Russia: the wielding of state power not to achieve public good but to reward friends, punish enemies, and enrich connected interests. This approach directly parallels the transactional worldview we explored in Chapter 1, where his father, Fred, taught him that every relationship is purely a matter of winning and losing.

Under previous administrations of both parties, migration was treated as a complex issue requiring both humanitarian responses and security concerns. The system wasn't perfect, but there was at least nominal recognition—reinforced by both American and international law—that asylum seekers deserved humane treatment.

Trump replaced this approach with deliberate cruelty, designed to deter immigration by making the process as painful as possible. As one senior administration official told the *Washington Post*, Trump loved the idea of people being "afraid of coming."[4]

This cruelty was first manifested in his first term's "zero tolerance" family separation, which tore more than 5,500 children from their parents with no adequate system to track them.[5] Nearly a thousand of those children the first Trump administration trafficked into shady "Christian" adoption schemes remain missing.

Underpinning these barbarous policies was a web of private contractors eager to profit. GEO Group and CoreCivic saw revenues soar, making over $1.3 billion from ICE contracts in 2019 alone. GEO Group's stock nearly doubled in the months after Trump's 2016 election.[6]

Caliburn International, operating the largest detention center for migrant children in Homestead, Florida, charged the government $775 per day per child, roughly three times the cost of a room at the Trump International Hotel in Washington. Not coincidentally, Trump's former chief of staff, John Kelly, joined Caliburn's board shortly after leaving the White House.[7]

These corporations didn't just passively benefit: they actively lobbied for harsher policies. GEO Group and CoreCivic spent $4.5 million on federal lobbying during Trump's first presidency and donated hundreds of thousands to his inauguration and Republican campaigns. CoreCivic's CEO told investors in 2019 that the company expected "meaningful growth" due to immigration detention needs.[8]

The perverse incentives were obvious. Private detention companies had every reason to maximize detainee numbers, minimize spending on care, lobby for harsher policies, and fight alternatives to detention, even when those alternatives were more humane and cost-effective.

Internal documents from GEO Group revealed the company targeted an "occupancy rate" of 95 percent in immigration detention facilities, effectively creating a corporate quota for human beings in cages.[9] This mirrors exactly how Trump, as we saw in Chapter 3, operated his business empire, prioritizing the *appearance* of success and short-term profit over long-term sustainability or human welfare.

This wasn't merely corruption in the conventional sense. It was, even worse, the systematic repurposing of government power to serve private interests, transforming human suffering from a problem to be solved into a profitable commodity to be traded.[10]

The Authoritarian Profit Model

Jakelin's death illustrates a larger truth: authoritarian governance isn't just politically dangerous; it's economically rewarding for the right people.

Trump's presidency perfected what I call the Authoritarian Profit Model, with four key components:

Deregulation makes corporations richer by removing protections for workers, consumers, and the environment. Trump's first administration eliminated over one hundred rules on everything from power plant emissions to workplace safety, delivering hundreds of billions in savings to corporations while imposing enormous costs on public health. His second term immediately restarted this process, with his EPA administrator announcing what the agency called "the most consequential day of deregulation in U.S. history" in March 2025, targeting dozens of environmental rules for elimination.[11]

Privatization shifts public services to unaccountable private firms, creating profit centers while reducing democratic control. Beyond immigration detention, Trump expanded privatization in education (through DeVos's school vouchers), health care (through dismantling the ACA), and infrastructure through public-private partnerships that socialized costs while privatizing profits. In his second term, this approach has expanded to nearly every federal function through the Department of Government Efficiency (DOGE), which is systematically outsourcing government operations to private contractors.[12]

Nationalism creates enemies who can be blamed for problems actually caused by corporate exploitation. By demonizing immigrants, Muslims, and "disloyal" Americans, Trump created pretexts for military spending, border militarization, and surveillance, all massive profit centers for contractor-donors. This technique draws directly from Roy Cohn's playbook, as we saw in Chapter 2, where creating enemies serves as both distraction and justification for consolidating power.[13]

Crisis exploitation uses real or manufactured emergencies to override democratic processes and fast-track controversial policies. Whether declaring "national emergencies" for border wall construction or using COVID-19 to suspend environmental regulations, the Trump administration repeatedly used crises as cover for actions that would face significant opposition under normal circumstances.[14]

Trump didn't stumble into this model. He inherited its architecture from decades of neoliberal policy beginning with Reagan, which increasingly subordinated democratic governance to market forces. (Louise jokes that when I die, she'll put "It all started with Reagan!" on my tombstone.)

What distinguished Trump was his willingness to strip away pretense. No more dog whistles or pretending tax cuts for the wealthy would somehow benefit everyone through "trickle-down" effects. Instead, he turned cruelty into performance, using public displays of dominance to thrill his base while distracting from the wholesale transfer of wealth happening behind the curtain.

As Adam Serwer memorably put it in *The Atlantic*: "The cruelty is the point."[15] But what Serwer missed was the profitability of that cruelty, serving as both a spectacle for the masses and an enrichment vehicle for GOP-aligned elites.

The Pandemic: Profiting from Catastrophe

If any doubts remained about the Trump administration's prioritization of profit over human life, the COVID-19 pandemic erased them. The worst public health crisis since 1918 became a case study in how authoritarian governance transforms collective tragedy into private gain.

Trump's incompetence and focus on the 2020 election gave America the highest per capita death rate of any major country. Over a million Americans died, almost half unnecessarily, according to *The Lancet*.[16]

He intentionally downplayed the virus's lethality, comparing it to seasonal flu while privately admitting to Bob Woodward it was "deadly stuff."[17] He mocked masks, promoted unproven treatments, and pushed for premature reopening against expert advice.

While ordinary Americans suffered unprecedented health and economic devastation, for certain segments—particularly those with Trump administration connections—the pandemic was an extraordinary profit opportunity:

- American billionaires gained over $1.1 trillion between March and December 2020, a 40 percent increase during a period when millions lost jobs, health care, and homes.[18]

- Pharmaceutical companies received billions in public funding to develop vaccines with minimal conditions. Moderna, for example, received $2.5 billion in taxpayer money, then patented a COVID vaccine developed with significant contributions from NIH scientists and priced it for maximum profit.[19]

- Well-connected businesses received billions through the Paycheck Protection Program while small businesses were shut out. Companies linked to Trump family members, administration officials, and donors received millions.[20]

Meanwhile, oversight was systematically obstructed. Trump removed the inspector general tasked with overseeing the $2 trillion CARES Act, limited the congressionally created Pandemic Response Accountability Committee, and refused to comply with transparency requirements.[21]

The more chaos Trump created, the more predictable the markets became for those with inside information. Several senators sold stocks after receiving classified briefings before the public understood the pandemic's severity. Cabinet officials and White House staff had unprecedented access to policy decisions and market-moving information.[22]

The pandemic revealed in the starkest terms that the authoritarian profit model doesn't just corrode democracy: it kills people. Literally, measurably, and unnecessarily.

Climate Sabotage for Profit

Trump's climate policies revealed how the same model applies to slow-moving catastrophes. He initiated the most comprehensive rollback of environmental protections in American history, eliminating over one hundred environmental rules including major climate policies like the Clean Power Plan. He pulled America out of the Paris Climate Agreement, making us the only nation to withdraw from this landmark effort.[23]

These weren't ideological decisions but economically motivated acts of environmental sabotage, designed to benefit industries that had heavily funded Republican campaigns. Oil, gas, and coal companies saw record access and influence. Coal magnate Robert Murray, who donated $300,000 to Trump's inauguration, provided an "action plan" that became a blueprint for environmental rollbacks.[24]

The financial benefits for these industries were immediate and substantial, while the costs were socialized: borne by communities suffering from increased pollution, workers exposed to toxic chemicals, future generations facing a hostile climate, and vulnerable populations already on the front lines of climate change.[25]

Indigenous communities like the Standing Rock Sioux saw their lands threatened by expedited pipeline approvals. Predominantly Black and Latino "fence-line communities" near industrial facilities experienced increased toxic emissions as enforcement actions against polluters plummeted.[26]

In a functioning democracy, the overwhelming public interest in environmental protection would have prevailed over the narrow interests of polluting industries. But in Trump's America, only shareholder value and campaign contributions mattered, even at the expense of planetary habitability.

His second term has accelerated this pattern. Not only are environmental regulations being eliminated at unprecedented speed, but climate scientists have been systematically purged from the EPA, NOAA, and the Department of the Interior, replaced by industry lobbyists. The very phrase "climate change" has been scrubbed from government websites and communications, as if eliminating the words could eliminate the reality.

Weaponizing the Military and Surveillance State

One of the most reliable profit centers in the authoritarian playbook is what Eisenhower termed the military-industrial complex. Trump, despite occasional rhetorical gestures toward reducing foreign commitments, proved exceptionally skilled at channeling taxpayer dollars to this sector.

During his first presidency, defense spending rose to $740 billion, the highest level since World War II when adjusted for inflation. The five largest defense contractors received over $150 billion in Pentagon contracts in fiscal year 2020 alone.[27]

The administration pushed through controversial arms sales to Saudi Arabia, the UAE, and other regimes with troubling human rights records, overriding congressional objections. The grateful Saudis later funded Trump's son-in-law's investment firm with $2 billion.[28]

What distinguished Trump's approach was the increasing militarization of domestic policy, deploying weapons and surveillance technologies developed for warfare against American civilians, particularly immigrants and protesters.

Border security became a lucrative frontier for the military-industrial complex. The "border wall" was less about migration management than channeling billions to contractors like Fisher Sand & Gravel, whose CEO pitched Trump directly on *Fox News*.[29]

Beyond physical barriers, the border region became a testing ground for surveillance technologies from companies like Palantir, which received over $1.5 billion in government contracts during Trump's first presidency. These technologies—including facial recognition, drone surveillance, and predictive analytics—were deployed against migrants before expanding to monitor protesting citizens.[30]

This militarized approach reached its apex during racial justice protests following George Floyd's murder. When demonstrations erupted in Washington, DC. Trump deployed National Guard troops, Border Patrol tactical units, and unidentified federal officers who used tear gas and rubber bullets against peaceful protesters, all for a presidential photo opportunity. In Portland, federal officers with no identification drove around in panel vans, snatching protesters off the street.[31]

This wasn't just political theater; it was a business opportunity for companies producing riot gear, less-lethal weapons, and surveillance equipment. As police departments nationwide received federal funding for military equipment, companies manufacturing tear gas, Tasers, and surveillance systems saw surging demand.[32]

In Trump's second term, this domestic militarization has expanded dramatically. Facial recognition systems initially deployed at the border are being implemented in major cities.

Law enforcement agencies from ICE to local police departments have received expanded funding for surveillance technologies with virtually no systems to make sure they're being used ethically or even legally. The distinction between counterterrorism and domestic policing has effectively collapsed, with profit-seeking contractors supplying both sectors.

January 6: The Final Payday

Even after Trump incited a violent mob to storm the Capitol—the most flagrant assault on our nation from within since the Civil War—corporate America's response seemed appropriate at first.

Multiple companies issued press releases condemning Trump's role in inciting the violence while pausing political donations to the 147 Republican members of Congress who'd voted against certifying Joe Biden's Electoral College win. Those announcements generated positive press coverage, creating the impression of a principled corporate response.

But within months, the money flowed again. By August 2021, over sixty major corporations had resumed donating to election deniers, including Toyota, Walmart, Pfizer, and Johnson & Johnson.[33]

Political action committees from industry groups like the US Chamber of Commerce also quickly returned to funding politicians who had voted to overturn the election. Dark money groups continued channeling corporate funds to these same politicians without the reputational risk of visible contributions.[34]

CEOs issued vague but high-sounding statements about unity and democracy. PR firms crafted messaging that let companies appear concerned while avoiding any substantive commitments. Lobbyists worked behind the scenes to make sure these corporations weren't held to account, and the Republican politicians—who regularly voted for whatever the corporations wanted—remained unscathed.

This rapid reversion to business as usual happened, tragically, because in Trump's new version of America the greatest sin wasn't attempting to overthrow democracy; it was losing access to politicians who could deliver tax cuts, deregulation, and government contracts in exchange for campaign cash allowed by five Republicans on the Supreme Court.

That corporate response revealed what's commonly called crony capitalism or oligarchy. When forced to choose between protecting our democracy and political access, most major companies chose the latter. Their executives correctly calculated that the public would quickly forget their complicity while the profits they made from political influence—including contracts, subsidies, and tax cuts—would endure.

Why It Matters

Jakelin Maquin's tragic story is not an outlier; it symbolizes the post-Reagan, post–Citizens United transformation of American governance into a profit-making enterprise where the suffering of our fellow humans became a moneymaking opportunity.

Jakelin didn't die because of policy, but because that policy put profit over protection, cruelty over humanity. This happens when democracy is gutted from within and sold to the highest bidder, the ultimate expression of the crony capitalism we detailed in Chapter 5, where billionaire donors purchase policy outcomes regardless of public interest.

Donald Trump didn't invent this system. The corruption of our government has been rolling along since the Reagan Revolution, accelerating with Reagan's neoliberal economics, corporate deregulation, and the post–Citizens United flood of money into politics. But Trump's administration perfected it, stripping away any pretenses that our government exists to serve the common good while hiding the nearly medieval machinery of exploitation beneath it.

What makes Trumpism unique isn't its corruption but its brazenness, essentially bragging that governance is just business by other means, that elected office should become a vehicle for private enrichment, and that human suffering is acceptable if it generates the right quarterly returns.

His second term brought this logic to its natural conclusion. When Elon Musk and the so-called Department of Government Efficiency (DOGE) began systematically dismantling federal agencies, it quickly became clear to anybody paying attention that it wasn't actually about efficiency, waste, or fraud. It was, instead, about removing obstacles to profit-taking while eliminating consumer protections, gutting worker's rights to unionize, doing away with environmental protections, ending investigations into Musk's companies, and discarding any other limits on corporate and oligarchic power.

The proof was right there in front of us all: nobody was arrested or prosecuted for fraud; firing people, like the 7,000 removed from the Social Security Administration, couldn't possibly have increased efficiency (instead, the program was made less efficient); and not a single clear item of "waste" has yet been identified (unless you consider saving the lives of starving African children "waste").

The brazenness of this scam forces us to confront this truth head-on: that authoritarianism isn't just dangerous but profitable, that democracy's decline has powerful economic beneficiaries who will resist its restoration, and that oligarchs will lie to achieve their goals. If we fail to recognize these simple lessons, we'll continue to live in a nation where the next Jakelin dies in silence at the same time quarterly profits soar in part because of her death.

The greatest threat American democracy faces today isn't any single leader, political party, or even ideology. Instead, it's the systematic subordination of democracy to market forces by a nakedly corrupt administration that views our constitutional system as quaint but archaic. It's the belief that everything, including free speech, liberty, and even basic constitutional human rights, should only be available to the highest bidder among the nation's wealthy.

This is the machinery that made Trump possible, facilitated by five Republicans on the Supreme Court and a supine media. And now in his second term, the contraption is running at full speed, steadily eating and disposing of what remains of the rule of law, democracy, and human decency.

As we'll see in Chapter 8, this profit-driven erosion of democracy and our basic rights inevitably leads to America being captured by our nation's oligarchs and their foreign allies, a situation where the public interest collapses while for-profit interests thrive. And as Chapter 9 will demonstrate, this domestic corruption then becomes an internationalized strategy, with wannabe autocrats worldwide learning from and reinforcing Trump's approach.

The billionaire donors described in Chapter 5 didn't just fund

Trump's campaigns: they funded this entire transformation of governance from public service into private profit centers. And unless we confront and dismantle this machinery, Trump may indeed become what Chapter 11 warns of: the last American president to be elected by a truly democratic system.

CHAPTER 7

From Birtherism to the Big Lie

Believe in truth. To abandon facts is to abandon freedom. If nothing is true, then no one can criticize power, because there is no basis upon which to do so. If nothing is true, then all is spectacle. —Timothy Snyder, *On Tyranny*

Ruby Freeman just wanted to count votes.

She wasn't a politician or activist. She was a sixty-two-year-old grandmother running a small fashion boutique called "Lady Ruby's Unique Treasures" in suburban Atlanta. In fall 2020, seeking to do her civic duty during a pandemic that kept many older poll workers home, she took a temporary job with Fulton County's election office. Her daughter, Wandrea "Shaye" Moss, had worked for the county elections department for a decade, and Ruby was proud to join her in supporting the democratic process, something particularly meaningful to her as a Black woman whose ancestors had been denied the right to vote.

"I've always been told by my father how important it is to vote," Freeman later testified before the January 6th Committee, "and how people before me, a lot of people, older people in my family, did not have that right."[1]

On Election Day and the days that followed, Ruby and Shaye worked long shifts at State Farm Arena, processing ballots with care and precision. It was the unglamorous but essential work of democracy.

Then Donald Trump lost Georgia, the first Republican presidential candidate to do so since 1992. What followed was a targeted campaign of lies so vicious, so persistent, and so personal that it destroyed Ruby Freeman's life and nearly broke American democracy itself.

I've seen a lot in my decades as a political commentator and activist, but nothing prepared me for watching an American president use the machinery of right-wing media to target ordinary citizens doing their civic duty. This wasn't just politics; it was deliberate character assassination with real victims.

Trump's allies, including his personal attorney Rudy Giuliani, seized on surveillance footage from State Farm Arena, falsely claiming it showed election workers committing fraud. The video actually showed normal ballot processing, but Giuliani presented deceptively edited clips to Georgia state senators, alleging workers had pulled "suitcases" of illegal ballots from under tables after observers were sent home.[2]

State investigators, including those working for Republican officials, quickly determined the "suitcases" were standard ballot containers and all protocols had been followed properly.[3] But by that time, facts didn't matter. Ruby Freeman and Shaye Moss had been selected as targets in service of a larger lie, the false claim that the 2020 election had been stolen from Donald Trump.

Trump himself mentioned Ruby Freeman by name eighteen times in his infamous January 2, 2021, phone call with Georgia Secretary of State Brad Raffensperger, calling her "a professional vote scammer," "a hustler," and "known scammer" without a shred of evidence.[4] Giuliani told Georgia legislators that Freeman and Moss were passing "USB ports" to each other "like they were vials of heroin or cocaine." The object referred to in this racist screed was actually a ginger mint.[5]

Right-wing media outlets published dozens of false stories about Freeman and Moss. Online mobs doxxed Freeman, publishing her phone number, address, and photos of her license plate. White supremacist groups sent death threats. Armed "protesters" surrounded her home.

On January 6, 2021—the day of the Capitol insurrection—the FBI called Freeman and told her to leave her home immediately; they had information that people were headed to her address. She didn't return home for two months.[6]

"I've lost my name, and I've lost my reputation," Freeman testified. "I've lost my sense of security, all because a group of people, starting with Number 45 and his ally Rudy Giuliani, decided to scapegoat me and my daughter, Shaye, to push their own lies about how the presidential election was stolen."[7]

The trauma was so severe that both women changed their appearances, moved repeatedly, and stopped using their names in public. Moss quit her job. Freeman's business collapsed. Both became virtual prisoners, afraid to go to the grocery store, to the pharmacy, or even to walk their dogs.

"I don't want to be a citizen of the United States anymore," Freeman told the committee. "Now I question everything. All because I did my job."

This is one small part of what Trump's lies did.

The Industrialization of Lying

Trump didn't invent political lying; in all probability, every president has lied at some time. Lyndon Johnson lied about Vietnam. Richard Nixon lied about Watergate. Bill Clinton lied about his affair. But these were defensive lies, attempts to cover up mistakes or misdeeds.

Trump did something fundamentally different, something we've never seen in American politics: he industrialized lying, transforming it from an occasional defensive tactic into a constant, offensive strategy.

Where previous politicians lied to cover mistakes, Trump used lies as a central governing tool to shape reality itself, to build a cult of personality immune to contradictory facts, and to systematically destroy accountability mechanisms that might constrain his power.

The scope was unprecedented. The *Washington Post* documented 30,573 false or misleading claims during Trump's presidency, an average of 21 falsehoods per day, increasing to 39 per day in his final year.[8] This wasn't accidental. It was strategic.

Trump understood that in today's fractured media ecosystem, with social media's top-secret algorithms prioritizing engagement over accuracy and audiences self-sorting into ideological silos, lies could serve as a form of tribal identity. By getting supporters to believe obvious falsehoods, he severed their connection to our collective shared reality and bound them more tightly to him. Believing the lie became an act of loyalty, a way of signaling commitment to Trump and his movement.

As historian Timothy Snyder observed, "Post-truth is pre-fascism."[9] By destroying the basis for shared factual understanding, Trump cleared the ground for authoritarian governance, creating conditions where power alone, not verifiable reality, determines what is accepted as true.

And the Republican Party, rather than checking this assault on truth, largely followed Trump's lead. From elected officials to right-wing media to rank-and-file voters, the party that once prided itself on clear-eyed realism embraced what Trump's spokeswoman Kellyanne Conway called "alternative facts."[10]

The result is a movement built on foundational falsehoods, engineered not to persuade through reasoned argument but to inflame through emotional manipulation, to divide Americans into warring realities, and ultimately to dominate through raw power unconstrained by factual accountability.

This machinery of lies didn't emerge fully formed. It evolved from a single, powerful falsehood that launched Trump's political career and served as a prototype for the bigger, more destructive lies to come.

Birtherism: The Original Sin

I remember watching in disbelief in 2011 as Donald Trump, then just a reality TV star and failed casino magnate, began aggressively promoting the false claim that Barack Obama was not a natural-born citizen and therefore held office illegitimately. Though "birtherism" had circulated in fringe corners of the internet since Obama's 2008 campaign, Trump used his celebrity and media platform to inject it directly into mainstream discourse.

"I'm starting to think that he was not born here," Trump declared on ABC's *The View*, adding falsely that "nobody from those early years remembers him." On NBC's *Today* show, he claimed, "I'm starting to wonder myself whether or not he was born in this country."[11]

None of these claims had factual basis. Obama had released his short-form birth certificate during the 2008 campaign, and his birth announcement had appeared in Honolulu newspapers when he was born in 1961. Even the former Republican governor of Hawaii Linda Lingle had confirmed the validity of his birth records.

But Trump wasn't interested in facts. He was testing a political strategy, one that combined racial grievance, conspiracy thinking, and attacks on institutional legitimacy. Birtherism offered white conservatives a way to express racial resentment toward a Black president without explicit racism, to justify opposition to Obama as based not on prejudice but on constitutional principle.

In April 2011, exasperated by persistent questioning, Obama released his long-form birth certificate. At a press conference, he said, "We do not have time for this kind of silliness. . . . We've got better stuff to do."[12]

Most politicians would have acknowledged error and moved on but, true to his Roy Cohn training, Trump did the opposite. He claimed victory while continuing to cast doubt, telling CNN, "I hope it's true . . . but a lot of people have very serious questions."[13]

That moment revealed much about Trump's emerging lie-based strategy:

- Facts don't end the lie. Even irrefutable evidence becomes just another opportunity to raise more "questions."

- The liar claims victory regardless of outcome. Whether proven wrong or right, Trump always positions himself as the hero of the narrative.

- The lie's utility is far more important than its factual status. Whether Obama was born in Hawaii was irrelevant; Trump's (and the GOP's) real purpose was undermining his legitimacy and stoking racial resentment.

- Media coverage amplifies the lie. Even when news outlets debunked Trump's claims, they gave him enormous free publicity which spread the lie even farther.

This was the birth of what would later be called "Trumpism," a political approach centered not on policy or ideology, but on grievance, tribal identity, and the systematic replacement of factual reality with empowering fiction combined with a cult of personality worthy of Jim Jones.

Birtherism was Trump's test case, and America failed it. The Republican Party didn't forcefully denounce him. Mainstream media treated his claims as worthy of debate rather than immediate dismissal. A substantial portion of the electorate proved willing to believe a transparent falsehood that validated their preexisting biases and resentments.

It established the template for what would eventually become the Big Lie about the 2020 election and the 2025 Big Lie about Venezuela "invading" the United States: both were racism dressed as constitutional concern, conspiracy wrapped in patriotism, and truth treated as entirely optional in service of political power.

The Trump Disinformation Engine

When Trump entered the White House in January 2017, he brought with him a sophisticated machinery for manufacturing and disseminating falsehoods at industrial scale. Since his reelection in 2024, he's upped the game by eliminating any of the dissenting voices that characterized his first term and threatening the media in a way that would make Orbán or Putin proud. His tool kit is straightforward:

- Trump himself as the primary source, with his uncanny ability to dominate news cycles and capture attention through provocative, often false statements

- Social media, particularly Twitter (now X), Truth Social, and Facebook, which allow Trump to bypass traditional media filters and inject falsehoods directly into the public discourse

- Right-wing media ecosystem, led by Fox News but expanding to include Breitbart, One America News Network, Newsmax, 1,500 right-wing radio stations, podcasters, and numerous online outlets that amplify and elaborate on Trump's falsehoods

- Republican Party officials who, rather than correcting the record, often repeat and reinforce Trump's false claims

- Foreign and domestic disinformation networks, particularly those based in Russia, that recognize Trump's utility as a chaos agent and work to amplify his most divisive messages

Each lie serves specific strategic functions:

- Deflect blame for failures onto others, including Democrats, the media, China, immigrants, and even his own appointees when they're no longer useful.

- Rally the base by confirming their biases and resentments, particularly against "elites," defenseless minorities, immigrants, and Trump's perceived enemies.

- Attack critics and institutions that might constrain his power or hold him accountable.

- Distort reality to create a world where his claims of success seem plausible to his base and low-information voters despite contradictory evidence.

For Trump, truth wasn't a value to be respected but an obstacle to be overcome in the pursuit of power. As journalist M. Gessen wrote, "Lying is the message. . . . It's not just that both Putin and Trump lie, it is that they lie in the same way and for the same purpose: blatantly, to assert power over truth itself."[14]

This approach has had devastatingly corrosive effects on American democracy. By flooding the zone with falsehoods, Trump has created confusion and exhaustion that made many citizens simply give up on determining what was true. By attacking sources of factual information as "fake news," he delegitimized America's independent press which, as our Founders intended, serves as a crucial check on power. By promoting conspiracy theories from the Oval Office, he normalized fringe beliefs and brought them into mainstream discourse.

Perhaps most dangerously, he's created what former Republican strategist Steve Schmidt called "alternate realities" for his supporters: hermetically sealed information ecosystems where inconvenient facts can't penetrate and where loyalty to Trump is measured by willingness to believe and repeat his falsehoods, no matter how absurd or easily disproven.[15]

The Psychology of Mass Deception

What made Trump's lies so devastatingly effective wasn't just their volume or the platforms amplifying them; it was how they exploited fundamental vulnerabilities in human cognition. Cognitive scientists have long understood that once humans adopt a belief, they tend to prioritize information confirming that belief while discounting contradictory evidence, what psychologists call "confirmation bias." Trump's Big Lies tap directly into this psychological tendency, creating what social scientists term "cognitive closure," where the mind becomes impervious to new information.

This explains why showing Trump supporters factual evidence often reinforced rather than corrected their misconceptions, a phenomenon called the "backfire effect." Each attempt to debunk the lies was interpreted as further evidence of an establishment or "deep state" conspiracy, strengthening rather than weakening the false belief. As decades of research into cults shows, when identity becomes fused with a falsehood, challenging the lie feels like an attack on the person's very sense of self.

This psychological manipulation has deep roots in what political theorist Hannah Arendt observed about totalitarianism: "The ideal subject of totalitarian rule is not the convinced Nazi or the convinced Communist, but people for whom the distinction between fact and fiction (i.e., the reality of experience) and the distinction between true and false (i.e., the standards of thought) no longer exist." Trump doesn't just lie; he systematically destroys Americans' ability to distinguish truth from falsehood. And in that epistemic rubble, democracy itself cannot stand.[16]

The Big Lie and January 6th

When Donald Trump lost the 2020 presidential election to Joe Biden, he did what he had done throughout his career when faced with failure: he denied reality and claimed victory.

"We have won this election," Trump falsely declared at 2:30 a.m. on November 4, with millions of votes still to be counted. "Frankly, we did win this election. . . . This is a fraud on the American public."[17]

What followed was the most sustained and dangerous assault on electoral truth in modern American history. It was, unambiguously, a coordinated campaign to delegitimize a free and fair election through false claims, groundless lawsuits, and ultimately, incitement to violent insurrection.

Like most Americans, I watched in horror as this unfolded, but still found it hard to believe an American president would go so far as to try to overturn an election he'd clearly lost. The components of Trump's campaign were unprecedented in American history:

- False claims of fraud in key states, all repeatedly debunked by election officials from both parties, independent experts, and dozens of courts

- Baseless lawsuits, with over sixty filed, almost all dismissed for lack of evidence or legal standing[18]

- Pressure on state officials, including Trump's infamous call to Georgia Secretary of State Brad Raffensperger, asking him to "find 11,780 votes" to overturn Biden's victory in the state[19]

- Conspiracy theories about voting machines, including wild and utterly false claims that Dominion Voting Systems machines had changed votes from Trump to Biden

- Alternative slates of "electors" in seven states Biden won, where Trump supporters created fake Electoral College certificates declaring Trump the winner[20]

None of these claims were true. The 2020 election was, as Trump's own Department of Homeland Security called it, "the most secure in American history."[21] Hand recounts, machine audits, court reviews, and independent analyses all confirmed the same reality: Joe Biden won the election fair and square.

But truth wasn't the point. The point was to create enough doubt, enough confusion, enough anger to justify unprecedented actions to overturn the election results. Or, at a minimum, to so thoroughly delegitimize Biden's presidency that Trump could maintain his grip on the Republican Party and then return to power in 2025.

The Big Lie about the election of 2020 worked because Trump had spent years preparing the ground. He had spent years systematically attacking the media, had undermined institutions throughout his first term, and had conditioned his supporters to believe that only he could be trusted. We should have seen it coming: in 2016, he'd repeatedly claimed that any election he lost must have been "rigged," establishing his fraudulent narrative before any votes were even cast.[22]

On January 6, 2021, as we all watched live on TV, the lie turned violent. Thousands of Trump supporters, convinced the election had been stolen, stormed the US Capitol to stop the certification of Biden's victory.

Five people died in connection with the riot. Approximately 140 police officers were injured, many seriously.[23]

All of this violence—unprecedented in modern American history—was driven by a lie. Interviews with arrested rioters consistently revealed they believed they were responding to a stolen election, fighting to "stop the steal" and restore Trump to his rightful position. Many expressed shock when confronted with evidence that their beliefs were based on falsehoods.[24]

For hours, Trump watched the violence unfold on television, refusing to call for the rioters to stop despite urgent pleas from allies, staff, and family members. When he finally released a video message hours into the assault, he told the rioters, "We love you. You're very special," while continuing to claim the election had been stolen.[25]

Even after the Capitol was cleared and Congress reconvened to complete the certification process, 147 Republican lawmakers—including eight senators—voted against certifying Biden's electoral victory in at least one state, effectively endorsing the lie that had just inspired a violent attack on their own workplace.[26]

The January 6 insurrection represented the logical culmination of Trump's yearslong assault on truth. When lies become the foundation of political identity, when falsity is elevated over fact as a governing principle, violence becomes inevitable. People who believe an election has truly been stolen, who believe their country is being taken from them through fraud, who believe they are fighting for democracy itself can justify almost any action.

After all, wouldn't you or I do the same or something close to it if we truly believed an election had been stolen? Isn't that notion of illegitimate representation what the American Revolution was based on?

The Human Cost

Ruby Freeman and Shaye Moss weren't the only individuals whose lives were shattered by Trump's machinery of disinformation.

Election workers all across the country faced threats, harassment, and intimidation in scenes reminiscent of a third-world banana republic. In Arizona, Pennsylvania, Michigan, Georgia, and other battleground states, officials who had done nothing more than accurately count votes and report the results found themselves targets of online mobs, social media doxxing, protesters at their homes, and explicit death threats.

Philadelphia City Commissioner Al Schmidt, a Republican, received messages threatening his family after he defended the integrity of the city's election results. "You lied. You brought fraud. Your kids are now gonna suffer," read one message.[27] Michigan Secretary of State Jocelyn Benson had armed protesters outside her home while she was decorating for Christmas with her young son.[28]

Gabriel Sterling, a Republican election official in Georgia, made an emotional public plea in December 2020: "Mr. President . . . Stop inspiring people to commit potential acts of violence. Someone's going to get hurt, someone's going to get shot, someone's going to get killed."[29]

Capitol Police officers suffered both physical and psychological trauma from the January 6 attack that Trump provoked. Officer Harry Dunn, an African American who faced racial slurs and physical assaults during the riot, told interviewers that he struggled with depression and emotional distress as a result. Officer Michael Fanone, who was beaten and tased by the mob, suffered a heart attack and brain injury. Four officers who responded to the attack later died by suicide.[30]

When truth is erased and replaced with politically convenient fiction, people become collateral damage. When facts become optional and "alternative facts" gain currency, the most vulnerable bear the heaviest burden. When violence becomes the enforcement mechanism for lies, democracy itself is in peril.

The GOP's Faustian Bargain

In the immediate aftermath of January 6, it briefly seemed Republican leaders might finally break with Trump and reject the Big Lie.

House Minority Leader Kevin McCarthy said on the House floor, "The president bears responsibility for Wednesday's attack on Congress by mob rioters."[31] Senate Minority Leader Mitch McConnell declared, "The mob was fed lies. They were provoked by the president and other powerful people."[32]

But this moment of clarity quickly evaporated. Within weeks,

McCarthy was at Mar-a-Lago, posing for photos with Trump. The Republican Party as a whole recommitted itself to the Big Lie.

Why? Because the lie worked.

It worked as a fundraising tool, bringing in hundreds of millions from grassroots donors convinced they were fighting election fraud.

It worked as a base mobilization strategy, keeping Republican voters engaged and angry.

It worked as a pretext for voter suppression legislation, with Republican-controlled legislatures in nineteen states passing thirty-four laws restricting voting access in 2021 alone, all under the guise of addressing "election integrity" concerns that their own lies had created.[33]

It worked as a loyalty test, allowing the party to purge dissidents like Liz Cheney and Adam Kinzinger who dared speak truth about the election and the insurrection.

This wasn't driven by a genuine belief in widespread or even actual fraud. Multiple investigations by groups from the FBI to the media told us all that many Republican officials and right-wing media figures privately acknowledged Biden's victory while publicly claiming otherwise. *Fox News* hosts like Sean Hannity and Laura Ingraham ridiculed Trump's election fraud claims in private text messages at the same time they brazenly promoted those same lies on the air, costing Fox hundreds of millions in successful lawsuits.[34]

This embrace of the Big Lie—across the GOP, conservative media, and even the tepid reporting on mainstream venues—showed the world a coldly calculated political strategy worthy of Goebbels: the Republican Party's elders and elected officials concluded that truth was less valuable than raw power, that facts were less important than maintaining an intense, emotion-driven tribal loyalty, and that the sacred integrity of American elections was an acceptable sacrifice on the altar of political power.

Why It Matters

The biggest lesson we can carry away from this horrific experience is that the greatest threat to American democracy isn't some random foreign interference, any particular procedural weaknesses in our electoral system, or even the voter suppression policies promoted by the GOP.

Instead, it's the very real threat of an authoritarian domestic movement built on lies, funded by billionaires, enabled by cynical political operators and right-wing media, and believed by millions of Americans who've been systematically cut off from factual reality and instead live in media and social media bubbles.

From birtherism to the Big Lie, Trump and his enablers constructed, brick by dishonest brick, an alternative reality so powerful that millions now inhabit it fully, unreachable by fact-checkers, judicial rulings, or even the observable reality that's so obvious to the majority of Americans. Unless this machinery of lies (and the Supreme Court decision that helped create it) is confronted and dismantled, we all face a dystopian future where elections still happen but losers never concede, facts never overcome intentional fictions, and where (like in so many banana republics) democracy exists in name only.

The story of Ruby Freeman—an ordinary citizen who just wanted to do the right thing and whose life was nearly destroyed just for doing her civic duty—is both a warning and a call to action. Her experience tells us the human cost of political lies, highlights the vulnerability of individuals caught in the machinery of political lies, and the moral bankruptcy of today's Trump-driven Republican Party that's willing to sacrifice truth and lives on the altar of naked power.

"Do you know how it feels to have the President of the United States target you?" Freeman asked in her congressional testimony. Now we do. And the question we all now face as a result is whether we will allow such targeting to continue, or whether we will finally reject the politics of lies and reclaim democracy's essential foundation: truth.

PART III

The Global Damage

The Beginning: How Trump Lit the Match

Remember that all through history, there have been tyrants and murderers, and for a time, they seem invincible. But in the end, they always fall. Always. —Mahatma Gandhi

So far in this book, we've explored the making of a young Donald Trump, from the Queens mansion where Fred Trump taught domination as virtue, to Roy Cohn's ruthless tutelage in shamelessness, to the golden façade he constructed that (with help from NBC and Mark Burnett) masked a lifetime of business failures. We've exposed the machinery that propelled him to power: a Republican Party that back during the Nixon and Reagan years first abandoned principle for tribal loyalty, the billionaire donors who funded extremism for tax cuts, and a series of billionaire-funded right-wing media empires that amplify outrage over truth on an hour-by-hour, day-by-day basis into tens of millions of American cars and homes.

But Trump's assault on democracy hasn't just been confined to the territory within America's borders. His presidency is far more dangerous to nations across the world who embrace the ideals of our Founders;

it represents a tragic and disastrous surrender of America's role as the leader of the free world and the planet's number one defender of democracy.

In these chapters, we'll see how Trump's embrace of dictators from Putin to Mohammed bin Salman to Kim Jong Un wasn't just embarrassing or even incompetent diplomacy; it was the betrayal of America's foundational promises going back 250 years, and touched off a green light for autocrats worldwide. We'll see how he and the true believers in his administration actively sabotaged America's capacity to deal with crises by attacking expertise, purging scientists, rewriting history, attacking the weakest among us, and politicizing every institution he could get his hands on.

This damage goes far beyond routine diplomatic embarrassments or simple policy disagreements. When Trump stood beside Putin in Helsinki and sided with the Russian dictator over America's own intelligence agencies, he didn't just commit political malpractice; he signaled to every struggling democracy in the entire world that America was done standing in the way of the expansion of authoritarianism and neofascism.

When his people (and Elon Musk's teenagers) systematically dismantled the EPA and he abandoned the Paris Climate Agreement (for a second time), he didn't just set back climate progress; he actively and maliciously accelerated planetary destruction in exchange for profits for his fossil fuel supporters, with consequences that will echo down through generations of human suffering.

Just like when his COVID-19 response degenerated into a performance of denial, magical thinking, and forced Blue states to compete for PPE and resources, he's again revealing how quickly a government hollowed out by a cynical, profit- and corruption-driven sabotage can collapse into dysfunction that hurts (and even kills) its own citizens.

These failures—including his bizarre performance with tariffs in early 2025—aren't accidents or simple incompetence (although they contain elements of both): they're the predictable outcomes of an administration that views the American government and its civil service as an enemy to be subdued, expertise as a threat to be discarded, and the historic norms of democracy that generations of Americans shed their blood for as optional.

In Part IV, we'll confront the nightmare scenario of Trump's second term: the machinery he built, the norms he shattered, and the alliances he damaged that have led to a systematic destruction of democracy itself here in the land of the free.

What happens in this twilight of American democracy impacts every person on Earth. The global damage of Trump's presidency has only just begun.

CHAPTER 8

The Heist of Democracy

How America's Voting Rights Were Stolen in 2024

THE CORPORATE MEDIA KEEPS TELLING US THAT DONALD TRUMP WON the 2024 election fair and square. They're almost certainly wrong: Joe Biden was, in my opinion, the last fairly elected American president.

Democracy lost big-time on November 5, 2024. This wasn't because of fancy software hacks or the fever dreams of some convoluted China/Venezuela voting machine conspiracy, but through an old-fashioned, systematic campaign of voter suppression similar to the ones that characterized the fifty years or so following the collapse of Reconstruction. What we witnessed in the election of 2024—and the media still has yet to acknowledge—was Jim Crow 2.0, and it worked exactly as well as it did in the late nineteenth and early twentieth centuries.

How They Stole It: The Numbers Don't Lie

The story is actually fairly straightforward: if all legal voters had been allowed to vote and if all the legal ballots had been counted, Kamala Harris would have won Wisconsin, Michigan, Pennsylvania, and Georgia. Instead of a second Trump administration, Harris would have become our president with 286 electoral votes.

The US Elections Assistance Commission (an official government agency) data tell us the damning story: a staggering 4.7 million voters were purged from the voter rolls before the election, all on the false claim of "voter fraud," something so rare that you're more likely to be hit by lightning than to ever encounter it.[1] By August 2024, self-proclaimed "vigilante" vote "fraud hunters" had challenged the eligibility of 317,886 voters across multiple states.[2] When Election Day arrived, millions more were disenfranchised; the Georgia NAACP, for example, estimates challenges exceeded 200,000 people whose right to vote was stripped from them months before the election in Georgia alone.[3]

This was a coordinated national strategy, organized and executed by the GOP and several mostly billionaire-funded groups aligned with it:

- Over 2.1 million mail-in ballots were disqualified for minor clerical errors.[4]

- 585,000 in-person ballots were thrown out.[5]

- 1.2 million "provisional" (what I call "placebo") ballots were rejected without being counted.[6]

- 3.2 million new voter registrations were rejected or not processed in time.[7]

And here's the true obscenity, the kicker that the mainstream media refuses to even discuss (for a variety of reasons): these rejections weren't random. A state audit in Washington, for example, found Black voters were *four times* more likely than white voters to have their mail-in ballots rejected.[8] And that pattern repeated nationwide. In Florida, North Carolina, and Georgia, analyses showed that officials flagged Black voters' mail ballots at more than twice the rate of white voters' ballots.[9]

The KKK Playbook, Updated for the Digital Age

Georgia was the biggest test kitchen for the new Jim Crow cooking, with Governor Brian Kemp as head chef, a role he'd played in previous elections by purging voters when he was secretary of state and running for the governorship. First, they used what my old friend reporter Greg Palast calls "Poison Postcards": official-looking mail sent to targeted voters. When Georgians (especially young, poor, and Black or Hispanic voters) didn't return these postcards (which were designed to look like junk mail), they were removed from voter rolls, a purging process that five Republicans on the Supreme Court legalized in 2018 with the *Husted* decision. In Georgia, for example, the response rate to these cards was barely above 1 percent.[10]

Then came the so-called "vigilante" challenges. In 2020, Palast uncovered a scheme where Republican operatives challenged the voting eligibility of 180,000 Georgians. Deeper investigation revealed this tactic was based on a program first deployed by the Ku Klux Klan in 1946.[11] For 2024, the Georgia legislature changed state law to make it nearly impossible for election officials to deny these challenges, and the program went nationwide.

By August 2024, True the Vote and similar organizations had signed up 40,000 volunteer "vigilantes" who challenged nearly a million voters.[12] A documentary film shows one Republican official, Pam Reardon, who personally challenged over 32,000 voters. When asked if she had verified any of the challenges, she admitted on camera, "I can't go through 32,000 people. I was handed the list by True the Vote."[13]

The Mail-In Ballot Attack

Republicans spent four years demonizing mail-in voting after the 2020 election, and it paid off. In Georgia, SB 202 slashed the number of ballot drop boxes by 75 percent—but only in Black-majority counties—and locked them away at night.[14] These moves reduced mail-in and drop-box balloting (used by the majority of Democrats in 2020) by nearly 90 percent.

The attacks on mail ballots were particularly devastating because research consistently shows racial disparities in rejection rates. In North Carolina, multiple analyses found Black voters' mail ballots were rejected at more than twice the rate of white voters' ballots.[15] In Texas, after new ID requirements were enacted, the rejection rate jumped from 1.7 percent to 12 percent during the March 2022 primary, with minority voters bearing the brunt.[16]

Provisional Ballots: The Ultimate Scam

Perhaps the cruelest trick was the "provisional" ballot. If you showed up to vote and found you'd been challenged or purged, you were offered one of these ballots and told your registration would be checked. What they didn't tell you is that unless you personally went to your county clerk's office with ID and proof of address afterward, your ballot was likely trashed.

According to the US Elections Assistance Commission, in 2016, when 2.5 million provisional ballots were cast nationwide, a breathtaking 42.3 percent were never counted.[17] And Black, Hispanic, and Asian-American voters were 300 percent more likely than white voters to be shunted to these "placebo" ballots.[18]

The Deadly Math

When we apply the most conservative calculation to these numbers, the suppression factor in 2024 was at least 2.3 percent of the vote. That translates to approximately 3,565,000 votes that, largely, should have gone to Kamala Harris. With those ballots properly counted, she would have topped Trump's official total by 1.2 million and won the Electoral College with 286 votes.[19]

This isn't speculative: it's the cold, hard math based on documented evidence from our own federal government. And it's exactly what Republican officials designed their laws to do. As Texas Attorney General Ken Paxton proudly stated on Steve Bannon's podcast after blocking Houston from sending mail ballots during COVID, "Had we not done that, Donald Trump would've lost the election [in Texas]."[20]

America's Nasty Little Secret

The nasty little secret of American democracy is that we don't count all the votes. Nor do we let every citizen vote. Because America is the *only* advanced democracy in the world where voting is a privilege rather than a right of citizenship.

Since 2020, according to the Brennan Center for Justice, "At least 30 states enacted 78 restrictive laws" to make voting harder.[21] Why would legislators fight so hard to pass these laws if they didn't affect election outcomes? The answer is clear when you look at the map of states with the most restrictive voting laws: it mirrors Trump's 2024 victory map almost perfectly.

America deserves an answer to this question: Excluding the boost from Jim Crow vote suppression games, did Donald Trump win? The evidence clearly shows he did not.

What Happens Now?

Martin Luther King Jr. gave us our marching orders back in 1965, and they're just as important today: "Let us march on ballot boxes, march on ballot boxes until race-baiters disappear from the political arena. I want to say to the people of America and the nations of the world, that we are not about to turn around. We are on the move now."[22]

Democracy can win, despite the GOP's 2.3 percent suppression headwind. After the 2016 election, Palast and others exposed a cruel, racist purge program called "Interstate Crosscheck" that cost nearly a million voters their rights. The Reverend Jesse Jackson launched a campaign that successfully shut down Crosscheck. Joe Biden couldn't have won in 2020 without that victory saving hundreds of thousands of votes.

We need to organize now to end the purges, the vigilante challenges, the ballot rejections, and the attitude that this is somehow acceptable in a true democracy.

That fight starts with naming what happened clearly and honestly: Trump didn't win. Vote suppression did.

CHAPTER 9

America Ungoverned

The best lack all conviction, while the worst are full of passionate intensity. —W. B. Yeats, "The Second Coming"

ON A BLISTERING APRIL MORNING IN 2025, ELIZABETH ANISKEVICH stood outside a community center in Washington, DC, filling out yet another job application. Just two months previously, she was an attorney at the Consumer Financial Protection Bureau with what she thought would be a lifetime career in public service. Now, at thirty-nine, she's watching her emergency savings dwindle as she struggles to make mortgage payments on her DC apartment.

"I was completely shocked," she told a reporter for CNBC, describing the day she received her termination notice. "I didn't expect it to unfold this way. There's no information about what's going on with my benefits, or what I need to do with unemployment."[1]

Across town, Sarah Boim, a thirty-eight-year-old former employee at the Centers for Disease Control and Prevention in Atlanta, is facing a similar nightmare. "Your career is ripped away from you, with no money to move forward," she explained. Her mental health has deteriorated so severely that her therapist insisted she immediately see a psychiatrist for antidepressant medication. "I have bipolar. It'll mess up my life if I have an episode. So we're just trying to be really careful. I'm hearing stuff like that across the agency."[2]

These stories are replicated thousands of times across America as the second Trump administration wages an unprecedented war on the federal workforce and, in the process, a war on the very concept of professional, competent governance. As I and multiple experts on fascism have warned for years, this is what happens when an authoritarian mindset takes control of the levers of power: institutions are hollowed out, expertise is denigrated, and ordinary Americans pay the price.

The Great Unraveling 2.0

When Donald Trump returned to the White House in January 2025, he wasted no time implementing what his former strategist Steve Bannon had called the "deconstruction of the administrative state."[3] This wasn't just campaign rhetoric; it was a deliberate plan to dismantle the federal government's capacity to function on behalf of the people, leaving only its supports and subsidies for giant corporations and the wealthy.

The instrument of this destruction is the Department of Government Efficiency (DOGE), headed by billionaire Elon Musk, created through an executive order on inauguration day, January 20, 2025.[4] Within weeks, DOGE had deployed teams of tech industry recruits—many in their teens and twenties with no government experience or security clearances—to federal agencies, where they began demanding access to sensitive personnel and financial data and directing mass firings.

The sheer scale of the purge is staggering. According to the Office of Personnel Management, over 200,000 federal workers had been laid off between the time Trump took office and early May 2025 (as I'm writing this), and approximately 75,000 federal employees have been forced to accept "deferred resignations" or buyout plans.[5] In some agencies, the cuts are even deeper. The Education Department alone is eliminating nearly 50 percent of its workforce, more than 1,300 positions through reductions in force, plus another 600 through "voluntary" separations.[6]

This isn't a normal political transition or a routine government reorganization. It's instead a systematic effort to cripple the American government's ability to protect citizens, enforce laws, and deliver essential services.

The Human Cost

For federal workers caught in this purge, the consequences are devastating. In Philadelphia, dozens gathered in the basement of the Queen Memorial Library for what organizers call a "Federal Employee Transition

Workshop." Some had been fired only to be yanked back or told they could be yanked back. Others had been placed on "administrative leave" with no explanation. Several reported being terminated for supposed "performance reasons" despite glowing evaluations, and now can't prove their competence to potential employers because they've been locked out of their files.[7]

"They want us gone," laments a government IT specialist, "but they're making it so hard to get away."[8]

The impact extends far beyond the affected employees. A fifty-four-year-old suicide prevention case manager with the Department of Veterans Affairs—who voted for Trump in 2024—now carries guilt over his vote as he watches the administration's assault on his colleagues. "It's not about the layoffs," he says. "It's about a dehumanization of who we are and what we do. . . . We don't do it for the applause. We do it to serve our country and serve our community. You get into public service not for the money but because you want to be part of something greater than yourself."[9]

A federal manager and Marine Corps veteran described the paralyzing fear that gripped his agency. "People are afraid to make a move that could result in an email dismissal," he says. "It's heartbreaking. . . . I have been trained to be a leader, and Trump and Musk are not allowing me to do my job. It's micromanaging at the highest level."[10]

What's particularly insidious about the Trump-DOGE approach is how it appears designed to maximize chaos and suffering. As Russell Vought, now director of the Office of Management and Budget, said before the election: "We want the bureaucrats to be traumatically affected. When they wake up in the morning, we want them to not want to go to work because they are increasingly viewed as the villains."[11]

They're succeeding. One Department of Defense employee, a man who served his country with two tours in Iraq, told *NBC News* that his post-traumatic stress disorder was triggered to the point that he called a suicide hotline, then visited an emergency room at a veterans' hospital.[12] In the months since then, the suicide hotline lost much of its funding to Trump's cuts.

Expertise under Attack

This assault on the federal workforce isn't just causing personal tragedies; it's systematically purging the expertise needed for effective governance. On March 12, 2025, Trump's EPA administrator Lee Zeldin announced what the agency called the "most consequential day of deregulation in U.S. history," targeting more than two dozen environmental rules protecting the environment for elimination or weakening.[13]

Among the targets are rules limiting pollution from vehicles and power plants, regulations on soot and mercury emissions, and the "good neighbor rule" that regulates downwind air pollution. Most significantly, the EPA is preparing to reconsider the scientific findings on the dangers of climate pollution that have served as the basis for federal climate regulations, a move that would strip the EPA of its authority to manage greenhouse gas emissions at all.[14]

According to the Union of Concerned Scientists, these rollbacks "will leave the nation sicker and our air, water and soil dangerously contaminated" while "sacrificing human health for the benefit of private industry."[15]

The anti-science approach extends beyond the EPA. Trump's administration has laid off hundreds of employees at the National Oceanic and Atmospheric Administration and removed mentions of climate change from public websites. The administration has also issued executive orders with language that could block enforcement of state and local laws that restrict production or use of fossil fuels.[16]

A Government in Chaos

Perhaps the most dramatic example of the administration's destructive approach is the fate of the US Agency for International Development (USAID), America's primary international humanitarian organization. In early February 2025, USAID's website went dark, employees were barred entry to their headquarters, and all direct-hire personnel were placed on administrative leave.[17]

On March 19, 2025, US District Judge Theodore Chuang ruled that DOGE's dismantling of USAID likely violated the Constitution, writing that the destruction of the agency harmed the public interest by depriving elected lawmakers of their "constitutional authority to decide whether, when and how to close down an agency created by Congress."[18] But by then, international aid programs had already been suspended, creating humanitarian crises around the world.

Beyond direct firings, the administration has taken a more insidious approach to dismantling agencies. According to documents obtained by the *Washington Post*, DOGE developed step-by-step plans for carrying out Trump's order to purge diversity, equity, and inclusion initiatives from the federal government and over six months intends to expand that campaign dramatically to target staff who are not in DEI roles but perform functions that DOGE's young workers determine are related to DEI.[19]

This leaves federal workers in a terrifying limbo. Katherine Freeman, who worked as an administrative assistant for the CDC specializing in tuberculosis, received a mass email saying she had been fired because of her performance. She had been at the agency for just ten months.[20]

Legal Challenges Mount

Multiple federal courts have found these mass firings illegal. US District Judge James Bredar ruled in a case brought by nineteen states and the District of Columbia that the firings amount to a "large-scale reduction in force" subject to specific rules, including giving advance notice to states affected by the layoffs.[21]

On March 14, 2025, Judge Bredar ordered eighteen federal agencies to reinstate probationary workers fired through what he called "illegal RIFs" (reductions in force), covering probationary employees nationwide.[22]

US District Judge John Bates characterized DOGE's work as "opaque" when he ordered an official to testify in a lawsuit against the Trump administration. Shockingly, it was the first time anybody involved with DOGE was required to answer questions under oath from an attorney outside the government.[23]

Openly defying many of these legal challenges, the Trump administration continues to push forward with its agenda. The White House response to these court orders has been defiant, with Press Secretary

Karoline Leavitt declaring that "a single judge is attempting to unconstitutionally seize the power of hiring and firing from the Executive Branch."[24]

The DOGE Paradox

While Musk initially claimed DOGE would cut $2 trillion from federal spending—a figure even higher than the entire discretionary spending budget of the United States—he has repeatedly revised this target downward, eventually settling on $150 billion in April 2025.[25]

Even these reduced figures are highly questionable. According to NPR, DOGE's moves to cancel contracts, end leases, and push agencies to reduce headcount "barely dent the government's balance sheet." As of March 2025, for every dollar the federal government had spent since the start of the fiscal year, DOGE claimed to have saved about four cents.[26]

The disconnect between DOGE's stated goals and actual operations has led many to question its true purpose. Veteran Republican budget experts have said DOGE's cost-cutting efforts appear "driven more by an ideological assault on federal agencies long hated by conservatives than a good-faith effort to save taxpayer dollars."[27]

Bill Hoagland, a former Republican staffer and director of the Senate Budget Committee for more than twenty years, told Reuters, "The playbook has not been for the dollar savings, but more for the philosophical and ideological differences conservatives have with the work these agencies do."[28]

Adding to the contradictions, while Musk and his team demand budget cuts across government, funding for DOGE itself has soared to nearly $40 million as of April 2025, according to records from the Office of Management and Budget reviewed by ProPublica.[29]

Why It Matters

This is how democracies die; not in a single dramatic moment, but through the slow, methodical dismantling of the institutions that make governance possible. What we're witnessing isn't mere political disagreement or partisan policy shifts; it's a fundamental attack on the capacity of our government to function at all.

As I've written (and ranted on the radio) for decades, the corporate right has long dreamed of dismantling the regulatory state created during the 1930s' New Deal and expanded during the 1960s' Great Society. They've wanted to cripple government's ability to protect workers, consumers, and the environment from corporate exploitation ever since David Koch ran for vice president in 1980 on a platform of ending virtually all federal agencies except the military and the courts. Now, under Trump and DOGE, they're achieving large parts of this vision with frightening speed.

The consequences fall hardest on ordinary Americans who depend on a functioning government. When the EPA can't enforce clean air and water standards, communities suffer. When FEMA lacks the resources to respond to disasters, lives are lost. When the CDC loses key scientific expertise, public health is endangered.

But the deeper threat is to democracy itself. When a president can effectively nullify laws passed by Congress by refusing to implement them or by deliberately breaking the agencies charged with enforcement, the constitutional separation of powers is threatened. When career civil servants dedicated to following the law are replaced with political loyalists dedicated only to following orders, the rule of law itself is at risk, as well as the competence of government.

Sarah Boim, a former CDC employee who says her mental health has been affected by losing her job, put it best. Reflecting on the chaos unleashed by DOGE, she told a reporter for *NBC News*: "Taking a sledgehammer approach and having an unelected billionaire in my email is just insane. What are his qualifications for doing this? The government is not a startup; we have been in business since 1776."[30]

The battle over America's governance isn't about "big government" versus "small government." It's about functional government versus dysfunctional government, about whether we'll have a government of laws or a government of men, about whether we will remain a democracy or slide into authoritarianism.

Because when governance fails, people suffer. And that's a truth that transcends politics.

CHAPTER 10

Autocrats United

Tyranny, like hell, is not easily conquered; yet we have this consolation with us, that the harder the conflict, the more glorious the triumph. —Thomas Paine

IN THE STARK OFFICES OF KYIV'S CENTER FOR CIVIL LIBERTIES, OLEKSANdra Matviichuk and her team meticulously document war crimes committed during Russia's invasion of Ukraine. By early 2025, they've documented over 68,000 cases since Russia's 2022 full-scale invasion.[1] This Nobel Peace Prize–winning organization has tracked Russia's crimes against Ukrainian civilians since the 2014 annexation of Crimea.[2]

I remember watching Louise's face as we saw news reports of mass graves in Bucha: the shock, horror, and tears. "This is Putin's work," she whispered. "But Trump helped make it possible."

She was right. The bombs falling on Ukrainian cities have many authors, Putin chief among them. But they're also the indirect result of American acquiescence to autocratic power by Donald Trump, whose presidency marked the first major retreat from democratic values in modern American history.

The Autocrat's Apprentice

To understand Trump's deference to dictators, we must return to that mansion in Queens where Fred Trump taught his son that kindness was weakness, and the world was divided into "killers" and losers. These weren't casual encouragements but imperatives in a household where success meant dominance, not happiness or community contribution.

This foundation was reinforced by Roy Cohn's scorched-earth

tactics, detailed in Chapter 2, which taught Trump that appearance trumped reality, attack was always preferable to defense, and admitting error was tantamount to surrender.

As explored in Chapter 3, Trump's lifelong commitment to creating the illusion of success found its perfect political expression in his admiration for autocrats. Dictators are masters of façade, projecting strength while their countries crumble, building monuments while their people suffer. Their gold-plated palaces and carefully orchestrated displays of adulation represent the ultimate version of Trump's own gold-plated brand: power as performance, strength as spectacle.[3]

The Putin-Trump Partnership Deepens

It was February 12, 2025, when Trump held his first direct call—at least one that we knew about—with Vladimir Putin since Russia's 2022 invasion of Ukraine. Louise and I watched the news when the story broke, both of us shaking our heads in disbelief.

I thought to myself, this is *also* how democracies die, not with tanks in the streets, but with phone calls between a real dictator mentoring a man who desperately wants to become one.

Since that ninety-minute conversation, Trump's rhetoric on Ukraine has increasingly mirrored Putin's.[4] By April, Trump was publicly declaring that "Crimea will stay with Russia" and claiming "Zelenskyy understands that," functionally legitimizing Russia's criminal annexation of that territory in clear violation of international law.[5]

The consequences were immediate. Trump's envoy Steve Witkoff—a diplomatically naïve billionaire real estate developer with zero diplomatic experience—has now met repeatedly with Putin in Moscow without an American translator or experts from the State Department or intelligence agencies. He's been pushing a peace plan that would force Ukraine to surrender significant territory while apparently also (according to press reports) laying plans for a Trump Tower Moscow.[6]

It's a pattern we've all seen repeatedly since Trump first stepped onto the nation's political/electoral stage in 2015: autocrats praising Trump's ego while he surrenders America's principles. This isn't diplomacy: it's capitulation to a foreign power disguised as some sort of bizarre deal-making.

Corporate America's Autocracy Dividend

And make no mistake: autocracy pays, at least for the autocrats and their oligarch supporters. That's one aspect of the dirty little secret behind Trump's affinity for dictators; his corporate backers love how the autocrats he wants to become like crush labor unions, eliminate environmental regulations, and slash corporate taxes while giving them immunity from investigation or prosecution so long as they suck up to and continue to fund the "big man."

When Trump praises Putin, sides with Saudi Crown Prince Mohammed bin Salman after journalist Jamal Khashoggi's murder, or lauds China's Xi Jinping for making himself "president for life," he's simply voicing what America's corporate elite view as the natural order of things: hierarchy and money over democracy. (It's worth noting that the only democratic institutions in a corporation are the unions; everything else resembles an ancient kingdom with CEOs as kings and senior executives and board members as lords and ladies.)[7] American corporations have poured trillions into China (in addition to moving much of our manufacturing base there) despite its authoritarianism, profit daily from Saudi Arabia's repressive regime, and many continued operating in Russia even after its illegal annexation of Crimea in 2014.[8]

Take ExxonMobil under Rex Tillerson, for example, who had Putin's Order of Friendship pinned on his chest in Moscow before becoming Trump's secretary of state during his first term. His company lobbied the Obama administration aggressively against Russia sanctions following the Crimea invasion; those sanctions would have blocked a potential $500 billion oil deal.[9] During Trump's first term, the new president pushed to immediately lift those very sanctions.

This wasn't just a twisted, anti-American-values foreign policy; it's a naked business strategy. Trump's administrations—particularly this second one—represent the ultimate fusion of corporate and autocratic interests characteristic of nations undergoing the transition out of democracy and into kleptocratic autocracy.

The Helsinki Surrender

I also remember watching that shocking Helsinki press conference in 2018. Louise and I were as stunned as the rest of the world was while Trump stood beside Putin and chose the word of a former KGB spymaster and psychological warfare expert over America's own intelligence agencies. That wasn't just a diplomatic blunder: it was groveling submission that humiliated America on the world stage. The same man from Queens who revels in bullying leaders from smaller democratic allies like France or Ukraine folded like a cheap suit in Putin's presence.[10]

Standing beside the Russian dictator, Trump sided with Putin over America's own intelligence agencies—the world's best—on Russian interference in the 2016 election. It was a public display of fealty by the supposed leader of the free world, bowing to kiss the ass of an autocrat who had explicitly attacked American democracy.[11]

Trump's relationship with Putin (and other autocrats) continues to worry international and domestic observers. In March 2025, Trump and Putin began laying groundwork for a ceasefire in Ukraine, with international observers and democracy advocates both worrying and warning that Trump may accept a deal finalizing Russia's illegal invasion and forcing territorial concessions from Ukraine.[12]

What our corporate media consistently fails to report is how Putin's approach to governance—state capture by oligarchs, attacks on independent media, intimidation of the legislative and judicial branches, persecution of political opponents—has become the clear template for Trump's vision of America.

It's not just that Trump simply admires Putin; he wants to *become* Putin.

The Saudi Connection: Arms and Influence

Trump's embrace of Saudi Crown Prince Mohammed bin Salman (MBS) reveals his willingness to trade the interests of America for personal profit. When *Washington Post* journalist Jamal Khashoggi was murdered inside the Saudi consulate in Istanbul, the CIA concluded with high confidence that MBS personally ordered the assassination.[13]

Trump's response? He vetoed congressional efforts to block arms sales to Saudi Arabia and ignored legal requirements to determine MBS's responsibility. "I saved his ass," Trump later boasted to journalist Bob Woodward. "I was able to get Congress to leave him alone."[14]

Trump's relationship with MBS has reached disturbing new heights in 2025. In January, MBS pledged to invest $600 billion in the United States, which Trump immediately demanded be "rounded up" to $1 trillion, saying, "I think they'll do that because we've been very good to them."[15]

The quid pro quo became clear in April 2025, when reports emerged that Trump plans to offer Saudi Arabia an arms package worth over $100 billion during his May visit.[16] This comes despite MBS's continued human rights abuses and the kingdom's refusal to hold anyone accountable for Khashoggi's murder.[17]

More troubling still is how Saudi Arabia has become central to Trump's foreign policy, hosting talks between US and Russian officials and mediating international negotiations.[18] It's a perfect illustration of how autocracy's influence has metastasized under Trump: the country responsible for Khashoggi's brutal murder now sits at the center of American diplomacy.

The corporate media's coverage was tepid, presenting it as merely "unconventional diplomacy" rather than complicity in murder to protect weapons contracts worth billions to American defense contractors. The same pattern plays out with Trump's embrace of Egypt's el-Sisi, Turkey's Erdoğan, and other authoritarians, putting corporate profits above human rights and democracy.

The White Christian Nationalist Connection

There's another pattern in Trump's favored autocrats: they almost all use white Christian nationalism as a rallying cry against multiculturalism, immigration, and religious diversity.

Hungary's Viktor Orbán has become the poster child for this approach, dismantling democratic institutions while claiming to defend "Christian civilization." After Trump's 2016 victory, Orbán jubilantly declared: "We have received permission from the highest position in the world to put ourselves in first place."[19]

This white Christian nationalist agenda serves as perfect cover for the economic agenda of autocrats, concentrating wealth in the hands of loyal oligarchs while convincing average citizens that immigrants, minorities, and (Jewish) "globalists" cause their economic struggles, not corruption and crony capitalism.[20] By wrapping authoritarianism in Christian religious virtue, leaders like Orbán dismantle democracy while claiming to defend traditional values.

Trump also deploys this same playbook in America, using racist and Christian nationalist rhetoric to energize his base while implementing economic policies benefiting the ultra-wealthy corporate elite who fund his campaigns.

Kim Jong Un: The Nuclear "Friend"

Trump's bizarre fixation on North Korea's dictator continues unabated. In January 2025, he promised to "reach out to him again," despite their previous summits yielding no actual denuclearization. By March, Trump was publicly referring to North Korea as a "nuclear power," effectively abandoning decades of US policy by accepting Kim's nuclear arsenal as legitimate.[21]

What Trump doesn't mention is that North Korea has dramatically changed its posture since their last meeting, sending thousands of troops to support Russia's war against Ukraine and strengthening ties with China. Kim is certainly watching Trump's Ukraine diplomacy with keen interest, calculating how many concessions he might extract from a president desperate for theatrical "wins."

The Republican Autocrat Tradition

Trump didn't invent the Republican Party's fondness for dictators. Nixon embraced Latin American dictatorships, Reagan supported apartheid South Africa and set up strongman governments in Central America, and Bush rehabilitated Uzbekistan's murderous regime after 9/11.[22]

What Trump did was drop the pretense that these alliances had anything to do with "national security" or "strategic interests." He openly admires these regimes because of their authoritarianism, not despite it.

Republican leaders increasingly celebrate this shift. At the 2021 Conservative Political Action Conference (CPAC), they displayed a golden statue of Trump, that being a perfect symbol of the party's transition from a conservative political organization to a personality cult modeled on authoritarian movements worldwide.[23] That golden idol was no joke; it represented a party abandoning political principles for devotion to a single man.

The Autocrat Strategy: A Dangerous Pattern

These aren't isolated incidents: they represent a coherent strategy that prioritizes relationships with dictators over democratic allies. Trump's approach to foreign policy is fundamentally transactional, viewing international relations through the same lens as his real estate deals: whoever offers the biggest financial package gets the best treatment, regardless of their human rights record.

The pattern is consistent:

- Praise the dictator personally while ignoring their abuses.

- Focus on financial transactions over democratic values.

- Bypass professional diplomats in favor of inexperienced loyalists.

- Capitalize on American retreat to pursue personal business interests.

As one expert noted regarding Trump's relationship with Arab autocrats: "There's no policy process, there's no interagency process. You have the cell phone number of someone. . . . You can either make a call or WhatsApp and get stuff done, and that's basically the way they do business."[24] That's precisely the problem; democratic governance depends on process, transparency, and institutional guardrails that Trump consistently undermines.

Media Normalization of the Unthinkable

"Putin is a killer," Bill O'Reilly said to Trump in a 2017 interview.

"There are a lot of killers," Trump shot back. "You think our country's so innocent?"[25]

In a functioning democracy with responsible media, this statement alone—a sitting president equating America with Putin's murderous regime—would have dominated headlines for months and ended a presidency. Can you imagine if Clinton, Obama, or Biden had said such a thing?

Instead, within days the news cycle had moved on, the incident becoming just another "Trump being Trump" moment in an endless stream of normalized abnormality.

This is also how democracies die: gradually, to paraphrase Hemingway, then suddenly. The corporate media's failure to maintain any sort of prolonged focus on Trump's autocratic behavior and admiration for dictators stems from a profit-driven corporate media and social media system where outrage drives revenue, but sustained critique threatens access and advertising dollars.[26]

I see it on my radio show with a depressing regularity. Listeners call in stunned by Trump's latest embrace of one or another dictator, but within twenty-four hours, some new outrage pushes it from the headlines. This dangerous psychological numbing has set in even among those who recognize the threat.

American Implementation of the Autocrat's Playbook

Trump's embrace of foreign autocrats and their ways of governing their nations has become official US policy through:

> Information Control: Following Putin's (and Hitler's, Stalin's, Orbán's, and Mussolini's) playbook, Trump calls critical reporting "fake news" and labels journalists as "enemies of the people," rhetoric that leads directly to death threats against reporters.[27]

> Loyalty Tests: Just as autocrats demand personal loyalty above duty to the nation, Trump purges officials who show more loyalty to the Constitution than to him personally.

> Weaponizing Law Enforcement: Following the autocratic principle that law exists to serve power rather than constrain it, Trump repeatedly—and publicly—pressures his Justice Department and FBI to investigate opponents and protect allies.[28]

This isn't just rhetoric; it's the methodical installation of autocratic governance, enabled by Republican leaders who've abandoned principled conservatism for proximity to wealth and power.

The Grassroots Resistance

Despite this grim picture, there's hope. Americans across the political spectrum are increasingly recognizing Trump's threat and are mobilizing to protect our democracy.

Civil servants risk careers to blow the whistle on abuses. Judges—including many Republican appointees—uphold the rule of law against unprecedented pressure. Journalists persist in reporting truth despite threats. And millions of ordinary citizens defend democratic values at the ballot box and in their communities.

Oleksandra Matviichuk reminds us that our democracy isn't just a system of government; it's a mindset, a commitment to human dignity that must be actively defended. "Because it is not NATO that Putin fears, it is democracy. Dictators fear the idea of freedom."[29]

Why It Matters

When Matviichuk documents Russia's war crimes in Ukraine, she's representing a global community that is struggling across the world against rising authoritarianism on four continents.

Donald Trump didn't invent autocracy but he embraces it, legitimizes it, normalizes it, and has been aggressively importing its methods into our government. His embrace of corrupt dictators aren't simply diplomatic failures; they are, in fact, existential threats to democracy itself across the planet.

What kept tyrants in check over this past century was American leadership: the example of a nation committed to the foundational principles of democracy articulated by our Founders, fought and died for by generations of American patriots, with the awesome economic and military power we've built over the centuries to back them up. Trump has systematically undermined each of these democratic bulwarks, thus helping empower a global authoritarian resurgence that threatens to reverse a century of worldwide democratic progress.[30]

It's almost impossible to overstate the danger. When the world's most powerful democracy openly sucks up to or does corrupt business with dictators like Putin, Orbán, and MBS, it doesn't just damage America's standing: it emboldens autocrats and wannabe autocrats globally to crush dissent and loot their own nations, knowing they'll face no meaningful consequences from America.

The damage to our nation and the rule of law will outlast Trump's presidency. Democracies eroded, alliances frayed, and norms shattered can't be instantly restored by an election or even the impeachment of Trump. History tells us that the global balance of power, once tipped away from democratic governance and redirected toward authoritarian models, requires enormous effort to rebalance.

Fred Trump taught his son that the world is divided into killers and prey. Roy Cohn taught him that appearance matters more than reality. Trump's business career taught him that you can fail repeatedly and still claim victory. Putin taught him that lies and the corruption of business elites can work. And now, as president again, Trump is teaching the rest of the world's autocrats and wannabe dictators a deadly lesson: America is no longer democracy's defender. Instead, we've become autocracy's enabler.

This isn't just politics. It's a war for democracy's soul. And we're all on the front lines.

CHAPTER 11

The Climate Collapse Presidency

Climate change is the single greatest threat to a sustainable future but, at the same time, addressing the climate challenge presents a golden opportunity to promote prosperity, security and a brighter future for all. —Ban Ki-moon, former UN Secretary-General, Remarks at Climate Leaders' Summit, April 11, 2024

THE GREATEST EXISTENTIAL THREAT HUMANITY FACES ISN'T HIDING IN A military bunker or a terrorist cell. It's in plain sight: the accelerating collapse of our only home's life-support systems.

Trump's first term was environmental arson. He gutted the EPA, installed fossil fuel executives in key positions, shredded over one hundred environmental protections, and abandoned the Paris Climate Agreement.[1] Scientists were silenced. Research was suppressed. The words "climate change" vanished from government websites as if deleting terms could delete reality.[2]

When confronted about climate's role in the devastating 2020 wildfires, Trump smirked: "I don't think science knows, actually."[3] Tell that to thirteen-year-old Wyatt Tofte, who died in Oregon's inferno embracing his dog as he tried desperately to save his grandmother.[4] As our Western skies turned blood-orange, Louise and I choked from a summer of wild forest fires, and record hurricanes pummeled our coasts, Trump mocked renewable energy and praised coal.

But his second term has proved apocalyptically worse. By April 2025, Trump had reinstated his "Schedule F" executive order, purging government agencies of climate scientists.[5] His new EPA administrator—formerly chief counsel for a coal conglomerate—is suspending methane regulations, gutting emissions standards, and fast-tracking permits for drilling in previously protected Arctic wilderness.[6] The phrase "climate emergency" is now prohibited in federal communications, while years of expensive-to-compile government climate data are being systematically altered, hidden, or outright deleted.

Climate collapse reveals democracy's most fundamental challenge: can we save our planet for our children and grandchildren when fossil fuel profits demand Republicans force inaction? The answer is becoming horrifyingly clear as tipping points approach: permafrost is thawing, ice sheets are destabilizing, and ocean currents are weakening.[7]

These aren't distant threats: they're happening now, accelerated by policies designed to benefit the donor class while sacrificing everyone else.

This betrayal falls hardest on poor and minority communities. Environmental justice and racial justice are inseparable.[8] Studies consistently show that communities of color consistently face the highest levels of air pollution, toxic waste, and climate disasters while having the fewest resources to fight back. And to add further injury, Trump and Musk have now gutted FEMA.[9]

As droughts intensify, coastlines disappear, and climate refugees multiply, the social fabric unravels. Democracy requires at least a modicum of stability, but climate chaos breeds authoritarian "solutions." The Pentagon itself identifies climate change as a "threat multiplier" that endangers national security. Scientists warn we have less than a decade to halve emissions before crossing irreversible tipping points.[10]

Our children will judge us not by our tweets or culture wars, but by whether we protected their right to a livable planet. The machinery of climate destruction doesn't operate in isolation: it's connected to the plutocracy that captured our courts, the propagandists who poison our media, and the authoritarians who threaten our democratic foundations.

This is the ultimate test of our republic: Can we break the stranglehold of fossil fuel money on our politics? Can we choose a habitable planet over quarterly profits?

Time is running out, and the climate doesn't negotiate. Physics doesn't care about political convenience. Either we reclaim our democracy from corporate capture and dark money in politics, or we surrender both a livable planet and our system of government to collapse.

The Last American President

The only thing necessary for the triumph of evil is for good men to do nothing. —Edmund Burke

Hope is being able to see that there is light despite all of the darkness. —Desmond Tutu

May 2, 2025, was a bad day for the news. Trump proudly announced his executive order kneecapping NPR and PBS, both trusted sources of independent journalism, in a brutal rhetorical attack.[1]

"Government funding of news media in this environment is not only outdated and unnecessary but corrosive to the appearance of journalistic independence," he declared as he signed the order requiring the Corporation for Public Broadcasting (CPB) to "cease federal funding for NPR and PBS." And then came the slap, the insult that followed the injury, as he claimed that both outlets received "tens of millions of dollars in taxpayer funds each year to spread radical, woke propaganda disguised as 'news.'"[2]

Trump's message was clear: NPR and CPB had failed the sycophant test and were being used as a vehicle to indirectly threaten any other media outlet that was similarly independent.

This executive order followed, by just a few days, an attempt by Trump to fire three board members of CPB; the news organization fought back by launching a lawsuit to protect its funding and independence. But after lawsuits against all three major TV networks and MSNBC and CNN, along with an FBI investigation into the publisher of *Politico* for printing an article comparing Donald Trump Jr. to Hunter Biden, the message is unmistakable: speak out against Trump or his administration and there will be a price to pay.

You could call it democide by intimidation.

In the first three parts of this book, we've traced the making of Trump, including how his father and Roy Cohn taught him to be a "killer" with little regard for the rule of law. Billionaires, massive corporations, and dark money networks funded his rise, along with help from foreign governments hostile to democracy.

He rose to power by repeatedly appealing to the worst in us, including racism, xenophobia, and misogyny. And now, as dictators and wannabe dictators around the world enthusiastically watch, he's taking steps to dismantle the social welfare state, legal institutions, and liberal democracy Americans of both parties have carefully built ever since the days of the Republican Great Depression.

So, now comes the work before us, the necessity of confronting the authoritarian playbook that's worked so well in Russia, Hungary, Egypt, Turkey, and so many other countries around the world.

DOGE is deconstructing our federal government at the same time Trump is cozying up to some of the world's most brutal dictatorships. Senior officials in the administration defend indefensible practices like ICE agents hiding their faces, refusing to identify their agency, and arresting people without court-signed warrants.

But it's important to realize that authoritarians fear the power of ordinary people more than they do armies, and that's us, you and me. History shows that the fatal weakness of dictators and those who want to become dictators is their dependence on our silence, our compliance, and their ability to throw people into despair and silence.

Thus, there's hope. From the streets of Seoul to the town squares of Santiago, from the Solidarity movement I met with in Poland in 2024 to the mothers of the disappeared in Argentina, we've seen democracy repeatedly strike back against what first seemed to be overwhelming odds.

Will we be the generation that watches democracy die, or the one who fights like hell to save it?

CHAPTER 12

The Nightmare Scenario

Louise and I watched on MSNBC as President Trump, on April 9, 2025, signed executive orders targeting two former officials who dared to defy him during his first term.

"I think he's guilty of treason, if you want to know the truth," Trump said as he signed an order stripping security clearances from Miles Taylor, the former Department of Homeland Security official who had written critically about the Trump administration under the pen name "Anonymous" in 2019.[1]

Next came an order targeting Christopher Krebs, whom Trump had fired by tweet in November 2020 when, as director of the Cybersecurity and Infrastructure Security Agency (CISA, now gutted by Musk), Krebs had declared the 2020 election was "the most secure in American history" and refuted Trump's claims of fraud. In an act of pure malice, in April 2025 Trump stripped Krebs of his access to the Global Entry system that lets people speed through Customs when entering the United States.[2]

But these orders went far beyond those two men. The presidential memoranda also suspended clearances for any individuals associated with them including employees at SentinelOne, the cybersecurity company where Krebs worked, and personnel at the University of Pennsylvania, where Taylor had served as a lecturer.[3]

As Trump called Krebs a "wise guy" and a "fraud," Louise turned to me with the same look of dismay I'd seen on January 6th four years earlier.

"This is only the beginning, isn't it?" she asked.

I nodded grimly. This wasn't just about Trump settling scores: when vengeance drives policy, democracy doesn't just weaken; it can die.

"I Am Your Retribution"

People often asked me on my radio show in the months leading up to November 2024: "What's the worst-case scenario if Trump wins again?" That question is now, of course, moot. The worst-case scenario so many of us feared is unfolding in front of our eyes.

That sounds hyperbolic, I know. Americans have a hard time imagining that our system could fundamentally break. We've survived a Canadian/British invasion, a Civil War, two World Wars, the Republican Great Depression, and countless other crises with our constitutional framework intact. Surely, people say, we can survive one man.

But Trump isn't just any man: he's uniquely dangerous in American history. Unlike previous presidents who at least felt constrained by democratic norms, Trump—as we saw in Chapter 3—has built his entire identity on the *performance* of success rather than its substance. His presidency isn't about governance but about maintaining the *illusion* of winning at all costs.

And as we explored in Chapter 2, Roy Cohn taught him that institutions exist not to serve the public but to be weaponized against enemies. Trump combines these lessons with a complete immunity to shame that makes traditional accountability impossible.

This is the pattern constitutional scholars like Kim Lane Scheppele have documented in countries where democracy has been destroyed by elected leaders who quickly became autocrats. "Modern autocracy comes through legal means," explains Scheppele, who studied Hungary's constitutional decline under Orbán. "Democratic institutions are hollowed out from within while maintaining a democratic façade."[4]

Trump's first term was just the dress rehearsal, a testing of boundaries, a probing of weaknesses. He was learning. His current term is now the main performance: systematic, strategic, and utterly transformational. Unlike other presidents who grew into the office, Trump—shaped by the Queens upbringing we examined in Chapter 1—sees governance solely through the lens of domination. He told us exactly what he planned to do. Now he's doing it.

"In 2016, I declared I am your voice," Trump thundered at CPAC in

March 2023. "Today, I add: I am your warrior. I am your justice. And for those who have been wronged and betrayed, I am your retribution."[5]

That wasn't just campaign rhetoric. It was a mission statement from a man who, as we've established, views every relationship as transactional and every institution as a potential weapon. Now, in his second presidency, he has fewer constraints than ever before.

No More Adults in the Room

During Trump's first term, his most dangerous impulses were usually thwarted by staff who quietly ignored orders, slow-walked directives, or even leaked plans to the press. We know this not from conspiracy theories or news reports but from the people who were there.

General Mark Milley, then chairman of the Joint Chiefs of Staff, told associates after the 2020 election, "They may try, but they're not going to fucking succeed" in using the military to stay in power.[6] Chief of Staff John Kelly, Defense Secretary James Mattis, and others formed what anonymous officials called a "guardrail" around the president.

In his current term, those guardrails have been systematically dismantled, including the mass decapitation of senior levels of our military.

In April 2023, Trump's inner circle helped draft a 920-page manifesto called "Project 2025," published by the Heritage Foundation but crafted by dozens of former Trump officials. This document, billed as a "mandate for leadership," provided a step-by-step plan for consolidating power and neutralizing opposition that Trump is now implementing.[7]

The endgame isn't policy. It's power: unchecked, unaccountable, and wielded for personal gain and vendetta.

The Department of Retribution

The Justice Department was the first institution Trump transformed during his current term.

He'd made no secret of his intentions: He repeatedly promised to use the DOJ against his enemies, calling for the prosecution of those who investigated him. "They should be prosecuted for what they've done," he said of Special Counsel Jack Smith and Fulton County District Attorney Fani Willis. "They've violated the Constitution. . . . they're trying to interfere with an election."[8]

Project 2025 called for removing independence from the Justice Department and placing it directly under presidential control.[9] The goal? To institutionalize this corrupt vision. And, sure enough, in Trump's second term the DOJ has been weaponized. We are seeing:

- Prosecutors who investigated Trump facing retaliatory investigations

- Witnesses who testified against Trump losing security clearances, as exemplified by the April 9, 2025, executive orders

- January 6th insurrectionists receiving pardons while peaceful protesters and students who write op-eds face federal charges

- Critics like Krebs and Taylor targeted for official punishment, with their colleagues and associates also penalized[10]

This isn't speculation; it's what's happening right now. Trump's April 9th executive orders targeting Krebs and Taylor were the opening salvos of a broader campaign that we can expect to last—and get progressively more aggressive—for his entire four years.[11]

The End of Free Elections

Trump's most dangerous fixation isn't on personal enemies: it's on the electoral system itself.

After all, Trump's greatest grievance isn't that he lost in 2020. It's that he was stopped from overturning the results. He promised that next time, he wouldn't be. Now, in his current term, he's making good on that promise.

The infrastructure for election subversion has been under construction for years. Since 2021, Republican state legislatures have passed dozens of laws restricting voting access, particularly in methods and communities that tend to vote Democratic. But more ominously, many of these laws also change who counts the votes, replacing independent election officials with partisan appointees willing to overturn results.[12]

In Trump's current term

- Election rules are being rewritten to favor Republican voters and suppress Democratic ones.

- The DOJ's Civil Rights Division has been neutered, eliminating federal protection for voting rights.

- State legislatures are being encouraged to override popular votes if they don't like the results.

- Voter roll purges, gerrymandering, and ID restrictions have exploded, particularly in Republican-controlled swing states.

- Election officials who resist are being replaced with those willing to "find votes" when needed.

The Voting Rights Act—already weakened repeatedly by Republicans on the Supreme Court—is being further gutted through DOJ non-enforcement. Federal election observers are being pulled from problematic jurisdictions in former Confederate states. And the president's bully pulpit constantly undermines faith in elections themselves.

As Trump himself said during his campaign: "The only way we're going to lose this election is if the election is rigged."[13] That wasn't just a prediction: it was a threat. Either he wins, or the system is corrupt. There is no room for legitimate defeat in Trump's worldview.

And now that he's won a second term, what's to stop him from seeking a third? Or a fourth? The Twenty-Second Amendment limits presidents to two terms, but with courts increasingly packed with Trump appointees, a DOJ that serves his interests rather than the law, and a Republican Party that has abandoned principle for power, who will enforce this constitutional limit?

Already, Trump allies are floating trial balloons. "His first term was stolen by the Russia hoax and impeachment," one prominent supporter recently argued on *Fox News*. "The Constitution should count from his first legitimate term—which is this one."[14] Others suggest that "national emergencies" might require "temporary postponement" of the 2028 election.

Once democratic guardrails are removed, they don't easily return.

Red Caesar: A Dictator by Another Name

Trump's authoritarian aspirations aren't hidden: they're increasingly celebrated by his intellectual vanguard.

A growing movement within conservative circles, from Claremont Institute scholars to Project 2025 planners, explicitly calls for a "Red Caesar": an American strongman who rules through emergency powers, bypassing democratic constraints in the name of fighting what they see as cultural decay and internal enemies.

What makes Trump uniquely suited for this role is precisely what we explored in Chapter 1: his family dynamics shaped him to view the world entirely through hierarchies of dominance and submission. As we saw, Fred Trump taught his son that kindness was weakness and that the world was divided simply into "killers" and victims. This worldview—that all human relationships are zero-sum power struggles—is the perfect psychological foundation for an American Caesar.

The mansion in Queens where Trump was raised operated on a value system of acquisition, dominance, and zero-sum competition that stood in stark contrast to the social evolution happening in America during Trump's formative years. While the civil rights movement, feminism, and counterculture were reshaping society toward greater equality and social justice, the Trump household remained frozen in time.

As clinical psychologist Mary Trump described in her book, which we explored in Chapter 1, her uncle Donald's personality was formed in response to an "emotional desert": his grandiosity, his need for constant validation, his inability to admit mistakes, and his casual cruelty all adaptive responses to a psychopathic father who viewed vulnerability as unforgivable weakness.

These childhood lessons have now found their most dangerous expression in his approach to governance, where cooperation is seen as weakness and institutions are viewed not as guardrails but as obstacles to be overcome or weapons to be wielded.

And they're saying the quiet part out loud. JD Vance, now Trump's vice president, has argued that a president should "seize power" from the bureaucracy and ignore court rulings that limit executive authority.

He promotes the apocryphal story that President Andrew Jackson told Supreme Court Chief Justice John Marshall to enforce his own order with regard to the Trail of Tears and then ignored the ruling.[15]

Trump himself has embraced this rhetoric of emergency powers while ranting about supposedly existential threats. "We will root out the communists, the Marxists, the fascists, and the sickos that live like vermin in our country," he declared in October 2023.[16]

When a leader compares his opponents to "vermin" who need to be "rooted out," history leaves little doubt about what comes next. This language isn't accidental: it's deliberate signaling about who belongs in Trump's America and who doesn't. Who deserves protection and who deserves punishment.

Trump doesn't need to declare himself a dictator. He simply needs to act like one as long as no one stops him.

The Hungary Model: How Democracy Dies While Life Goes On

In July 2022, CPAC met in Budapest, with Viktor Orbán receiving a standing ovation for declaring that if the GOP wanted real power they had to seize control of the media, the courts, and embark on institutional restructuring. This wasn't coincidence; it was acknowledgment that Hungary had become the Republican template for America's potential transformation.[17]

Having been there and reported from there, I can testify that what makes the Hungarian model so dangerous is how normal it feels to citizens living through it. As Scheppele explains, "The case of Hungary shows how autocrats can rig elections legally, using legislative majorities to change the law and neutralize the opposition at every turn." Most critically, "it happened through paperwork" rather than violence.[18]

This is the "frog in boiling water" phenomenon where democracy dies incrementally while daily life continues. People still work, shop, watch sports, and post on social media. Each restriction seems minor until suddenly, they're not. At first, only critics and targeted minorities feel the full weight of autocratic power, creating powerful incentives for self-censorship among the rest of the population.[19]

The steps Orbán followed have become America's road map:

- Courts captured through systematic appointments

- Election rules reshaped to favor one party

- Media controlled through regulatory pressure

- Constitutional norms eroded systematically

- Society divided into permanent in-groups and out-groups[20]

As rights disappear, expectations shift. What once seemed outrageous becomes normal. The psychological accommodation happens gradually, with cognitive dissonance leading many to justify the new reality rather than resist it.[21]

This pattern is unfolding in America today, and, like in Hungary, it's a transformation by paperwork, not violence; it's happening while life appears normal. Until it doesn't.

The Compliance Apparatus

Beyond individual retribution, Trump has created institutional mechanisms to enforce loyalty. The blueprint had already been tested in states like Florida, Texas, and in Hungary under Orbán.

- Universities now face funding cuts for teaching "anti-American" ideas (defined as criticism of Trump or conservative orthodoxy).[22]

- Media companies face regulatory harassment, antitrust investigations, and they and their reporters and commentators are the victims of libel lawsuits.[23]

- Social media platforms have been given a choice: remove "anti-Trump" content or lose profitable Section 230 protections.

- Federal employees undergo "ideological vetting" with those deemed "woke" or "liberal" purged.

- Private companies face pressure to fire or blacklist Trump critics.

This system of enforced compliance doesn't require new laws, just the selective enforcement of existing ones. In autocracies, regulatory agencies become weapons aimed at enemies and shields protecting allies.

- The IRS audits Trump critics while ignoring allies' tax law violations.[24]

- The FCC targets networks like CNN and MSNBC with regulatory harassment while giving Fox News and right-wing media a free pass.[25]

- The SEC investigates companies that speak out against Trump's policies while fast-tracking approvals for supporters.

- Even local police departments feel the pressure, with federal grants tied to their willingness to crack down on protests against Trump while the general right-wing tilt of police departments mean they often ignore violence by his supporters.

This targeted enforcement creates a society where the law no longer protects everyone equally; it protects those in favor and punishes those who aren't.

The International Warning Signs

On the international front, the warning signs provoked by Trump's embrace of fascist regimes around the world are already flashing red. NATO allies are voicing concerns about the future of the alliance. Ukraine's government is desperately seeking assurances that American support will continue. Taiwan is accelerating its defense preparations as China watches developments in Washington.

These aren't speculative scenarios; they're the active, real-time responses of global actors to America's democratic instability. In diplomatic channels and across international forums, frantic discussions are taking place right now about how to adapt to a "post-American global order." Some countries are hedging their bets, strengthening ties with

China and Russia as insurance against US withdrawal from the world-wide family of democratic nations.

Trump's first term demonstrated his willingness to break with long-standing allies and embrace dictators. His current actions—praising Putin amid Russia's ongoing war, questioning NATO's relevance, and suggesting greater accommodation with authoritarian regimes—signal a continuation and acceleration of that approach.

Why It Matters

In a true democracy, to paraphrase Reagan, elections have consequences. When power changes hands, policy changes too. But what happens when the system is rigged so thoroughly that elections no longer meaningfully transfer power?

Consider what's happening in America today:

- State legislatures, gerrymandered beyond accountability, are passing laws giving themselves more power over election administration.

- The Supreme Court has already ruled in favor of expanded state legislature authority over elections, with more cases pending.

- Voter ID laws, purges, and other restrictions are being implemented with increasing precision to target Democratic-leaning demographic groups.

- Media ecosystems continue to fragment, with Americans increasingly consuming entirely different sets of facts based on their political alignment.

- Corporate money in politics is reaching unprecedented levels, with policy outcomes increasingly aligned with donor preferences rather than public opinion.

These aren't hypothetical future scenarios; they're underway right now. The machinery of democracy isn't destroyed overnight; it's recalibrated day by day. You can still cast a ballot. You can still enter a voting booth. But the system itself is being restructured to ensure predictable outcomes.

This is how America could see its last genuinely democratic president, not through the abolition of elections, but through their transformation—like in Russia—into ritualistic exercises that no longer determine who holds power.

For Americans who grew up in a stable democracy, this collapse probably seems unimaginable. But history teaches us that democracies don't usually die through military coups or dramatic upheavals. They die through step-by-step legal erosion, with elected officials and their bureaucrats and judges dismantling checks and balances while maintaining a façade of legitimacy.

It happened in Hungary under Orbán, in Venezuela under Chávez, in Turkey under Erdoğan, in Russia under Putin. Each began with democratic elections. Each ended with rigged systems where opposition became functionally impossible.

And each happened to a population that couldn't imagine losing their freedom until it was already gone.

According to Scheppele, the warning signs were clear in Hungary. "For a while, I thought, 'This would never happen here,'" she explained in a 2022 interview. "The biggest mistake that I made was a failure of imagination."[26]

Democracy doesn't announce its departure with trumpets. It slips away in silence, one compromised institution at a time. And Trump—backed by billionaires, amplified by right-wing propaganda networks, funded by foreign oligarchs, and protected by a captured party—has both the means and the motive to make America the next democracy to fall to secure his own safety and wealth.

The endgame isn't conservatism. It isn't, in fact, policy at all. It's a complete restructuring of American governance to ensure permanent rule by a single leader and party. It's the potential end of the American experiment in regular and peaceful transfers of political power.

This isn't about left versus right anymore. It's about democracy versus authoritarianism. And if we don't recognize this reality soon, Trump may not just be serving his second term: he could be laying the groundwork to become America's last democratically elected president.

CHAPTER 13

The Empathy Deficit

Democracy's Essential Ingredient

The social compact would dissolve, and justice be extirpated from the earth, or have only a casual existence, were we callous to the touches of affection. —Thomas Paine

IN JANUARY, AS ANOTHER BRUTAL MAINE WINTER GRIPPED THE NORTH-east, Dwayne LaBrecque faced an impossible choice. The diabetic father of five, who'd lost several toes and part of his foot to infection, stared at his most recent heating bill with a growing dread. After losing his job as a shipping manager, Dwayne's income had collapsed.[1]

For years, he'd relied on LIHEAP—the Low Income Home Energy Assistance Program created by Congress in 1981—to keep his family warm through Maine's harsh winters. But soon after his inauguration, Trump and congressional Republicans had put LIHEAP on the chopping block.

"If the president turned around and did away with that funding," Dwayne told a local reporter, his voice breaking, "I have no idea how we'd survive the winter."

His story isn't at all unique. Across America, literally millions of families face similar crises every year, from heat to food to housing to medical and school bills, as the Trump administration dismantles the safety net that has protected vulnerable Americans for generations. But what strikes me most isn't just the policy change; it's the profound empathy deficit that enables it.

During my years rostered as a psychotherapist back in the 1980s, I learned that there's a subset of humanity—roughly 1.5 to 4 percent of the general population—who lack the neurological or psychological ability to experience empathy. These individuals, often described clinically as sociopaths or psychopaths, process others' pain in a purely intellectual way. They recognize suffering but feel little to nothing in response. No emotional twinge, no discomfort, no moral imperative to help.

While they represent a small fraction of the general population, they account for about one-third of our prison populations, commit roughly 90 percent of America's violent crimes, and—most relevant to our current situation—are approximately 21 percent of all corporate CEOs.[2] This last statistic helps explain how the American government, with big money from these CEOs following Lewis Powell's infamous 1971 memo, has been transformed from an institution dedicated to the common good into something that increasingly resembles a corporate boardroom where human suffering is just an externality to be managed.

This mindset has now infected our entire system of government. It's why Trump gleefully kept Kilmar Abrego Garcia in an El Salvadoran concentration camp even in defiance of a Supreme Court order to release him. It's why he and his Project 2025 architects dismantled programs that helped vulnerable Americans without a twinge of conscience.[3] It's why his administration can watch climate disasters devastate communities while simultaneously rolling back environmental protections and gutting FEMA. This isn't just partisan policy disagreement; it's an empathy deficit elevated to governing philosophy.

This lack of empathy gets philosophical backing from figures like Nietzsche and Ayn Rand, both favorites among Republicans and Libertarians who view compassion as weakness. Nietzsche famously called pity "a waste of feeling, a moral parasite which is injurious to the health," while Rand built an entire philosophy around the "virtue of selfishness." It's no coincidence that billionaires like Elon Musk—who recently called empathy "the fundamental weakness of Western civilization"—find these ideas attractive. They provide intellectual cover for what is, at root, a profound moral failing.

Yet empathy isn't a flaw; it's the cornerstone of civilization itself. It's the foundation upon which our democratic experiment was built. The Framers understood this, which is why both the preamble and Article I of our Constitution mention the "General Welfare." Alexander Hamilton noted that "common interest may always be reckoned upon as the surest bond of sympathy." Thomas Jefferson and James Madison both emphasized that government must serve more than just the powerful.

As I detailed in *The Hidden History of American Democracy*, concern for *every* community member is what led tribal people around the world to create largely egalitarian political structures throughout prehistory, structures on which we based our own Constitution. Margaret Mead noted this, pointing out how the evidence of healed bones was a surefire sign that prehistoric people didn't leave their injured members to die but nurtured them back to health, even though the time and effort may have represented a risk to the tribe. Empathy built America and has guided our progress, in fits and starts but nonetheless generation by generation, toward a "more perfect union."

When this essential quality of empathy vanishes from governance, democracy itself begins to collapse. A nation without empathy isn't really a nation at all; it's just a crime syndicate with a flag and army, a conspiracy to use the powers of government—the only institution that can legally deprive us of our freedom or even our lives—to elevate the powerful while crushing the weak. This ultimate expression of governmental sociopathy is called fascism, oligarchy, or authoritarianism. But whatever the label, the substance remains the same: rule by those who view human suffering as abstract and simply an acceptable price to be paid for wealth and power.

This is precisely what we're witnessing now. As Trump implements Project 2025's blueprint for dismantling the administrative state, each policy change reflects not just different priorities from America's historic values, but a fundamentally different conception of what government itself is for. Instead of an institution that protects the vulnerable and promotes the general welfare, Trump views our government as a weapon to reward friends, punish enemies, and enrich the already wealthy, a machine of sorts for transforming public resources into private gain.

Dwayne LaBrecque feels this transformation most acutely. For him, LIHEAP wasn't an abstract budget line; it was the difference between his family sleeping in warmth or shivering through another Maine winter. But in an administration where empathy is viewed as weakness, Dwayne's suffering simply doesn't matter.

Why It Matters

This is the deepest danger of Trump's second term. Beyond specific policies, beyond institutional damage, he shows us what it looks like when sociopathy becomes a governing philosophy, a view of politics where the vulnerable aren't citizens deserving protection but "useless eaters."

Democracy can't survive this sort of empathy deficit, as Franklin D. Roosevelt pointed out when he said, "Better the occasional faults of a government that lives in a spirit of charity than the consistent omissions of a government frozen in the ice of its own indifference."

But as we'll explore in the next chapter, this isn't inevitable. Resistance remains possible. Reform is achievable. The democratic ideal of our Founders and most presidents since that time—a government of, by, and for the people—still lives in the hearts of millions of Americans who refuse to accept a nation without empathy.

CHAPTER 14

Reform, Resist, and Remember

Tag, you're it. —Thom Hartmann

Resist: How We Defeat Authoritarianism

The day after Donald Trump won the 2024 election, it seemed like every liberal and progressive friend I knew was either talking about moving to Canada or stocking up on canned goods, ready to hunker down for the inevitable descent into authoritarianism.

I get it. After reading the previous chapters of this book, you might feel a sense of hopelessness. The path toward autocracy sometimes seems inevitable because we've all seen the pattern repeated in countries that have already fallen. The machinery of oligarchy and autocracy is well-oiled, the morbidly rich are already largely in charge, the courts are captured, the media is under assault, and truth itself—particularly in the increasingly popular right-wing media and on billionaire-owned social media—is more often than not optional.

But here's our mantra: authoritarianism is not our destiny. Once we realize what's going on, it becomes a choice, and we can choose to reject it.

These aren't empty platitudes or wishful thinking. History shows us that authoritarians are often defeated. Fascists can be stopped from within. Democracy, though imperfect, can revive itself even after periods of right-wing darkness.

Consider the examples of South Korea in 2016–2017 and again in 2024. When President Park Geun-hye's corruption scandal broke in 2016, millions of Koreans took to the streets in peaceful protest. For months, citizens held weekly candlelight demonstrations that drew people from all walks of life. Those protests led directly to Park's impeachment, removal from office, and later imprisonment. There was a similar reclaiming of democracy when, in 2024, President Yoon Suk Yeol tried to make himself a dictator with state-of-emergency and martial law declarations. Like Park, Yoon was jailed and impeached and democracy has now returned to South Korea.[1]

Or look at Chile. After seventeen years of Augusto Pinochet's dictatorship (installed by Nixon and Kissinger with the help of four American corporations), Chileans organized, mobilized, and ultimately voted him out in a 1988 referendum that he himself had arranged, confident he would win. They defeated him with something as simple as hope, embodied in their campaign slogan "La alegría ya viene" ("Joy is coming").[2]

Similarly, in 2022, Sri Lankans from all walks of life—crossing previously unbridgeable ethnic and religious divides—united in peaceful protest to force out the corrupt and authoritarian Rajapaksa dynasty that then ruled their country with an iron fist.[3]

These aren't isolated examples. They're part of a pattern across history: ordinary people, fighting together with strategic focus and moral clarity, can and often do defeat authoritarians.

Understanding the Authoritarian Playbook

To defeat authoritarians, we must first understand their methodology. Their playbook is remarkably consistent across countries and eras:

- Divide the population into "real" citizens versus "enemies of the people."

- Attack independent media as "fake news." Corrupt the judiciary to serve power rather than justice.

- Capture electoral systems to ensure they can never lose.

- Militarize law enforcement to protect the regime, not the public.

- Rewrite history to create myths that support their power.

- Use economic anxiety to justify targeting vulnerable groups.

- Co-opt religious and patriotic symbols to present opposition as treason.

This playbook has been deployed in Russia under Putin, Hungary under Orbán, Turkey under Erdoʄüan, Brazil under Bolsonaro, and the Philippines under Duterte, among others throughout the history of the past century.[4] And, eerily, these steps are precisely the strategy Trump and his allies tried during his first term and are now pursuing in his second.

But here's the good news: because the authoritarian playbook is generally consistent, the strategies and methods to fight back can be as well. Successful resistance to authoritarianism, like authoritarianism itself, usually follows patterns we can learn from and appropriate for our own use.

Building the Resistance: Seven Strategies That Work

Looking at the history of successful anti-authoritarian movements around the world, here are seven proven strategies I've identified that can help us protect and revive what's left of our own democracy:

1. Unite across Traditional Divides

Authoritarians often win when they successfully divide the opposition, like Trump is trying to do by getting Americans to hate on their queer, brown-skinned, and well-educated "liberal" neighbors. The most effective resistance movements overcome these kinds of traditional political, ethnic, and social divisions by forming democracy-focused coalitions.

In Poland, as Louise and I learned when we visited in 2024, when the hard-right Law and Justice Party (PiS) attempted to capture the judiciary and media, average people across ideological lines from left to right rose up and fought back. Civil society groups that had historically disagreed on policy set aside differences to defend what was left of their democracy. And it worked. As our guide in Gdansk proudly told us (he'd participated in the street protests and even endured gunfire), that coalition ended eight years of authoritarian PiS rule in 2023.[5]

And there are signs the same is happening here. Progressives and traditional conservatives are finding common cause in defending democratic norms and institutions as we see with the Lincoln Project and other efforts, embracing the ideals our Founders fought and died for in the Declaration of Independence and the Bill of Rights. Urban and rural voters are increasingly coming together as we have seen in the regular anti-Trump, anti-fascism demonstrations that have shown up in virtually every town and city in America. All we have to do is set aside our policy differences so we can together preserve the system that makes possible the eventual policy debates we'll revisit when full democracy is restored.

2. Protect Truth and Information Ecosystems

Authoritarians succeed, as George Orwell pointed out in 1984, when truth is subjective and facts are controlled by the state. Thus, Trump's power, to a surprising extent, depends on his ability to control information and undermine independent sources of truth. This, of course, is why wannabe dictators always go after media early on.

Today, with right-wing-biased social media algorithms driving hate, polarization, and disinformation to hold eyeballs and increase profits, protecting truth requires both individual and systemic approaches:

- Support independent local journalism through subscriptions and donations.

- Promote media literacy in schools and communities (Finland has pioneered this).

- Create cross-partisan fact-checking organizations and websites that transcend political divides.

- Require transparency of social media algorithms that today profit from division and falsehood.

- Build and elevate media outlets that promote accuracy over eyeballs.

As philosopher Hannah Arendt noted, "Freedom of opinion is a farce unless factual information is guaranteed."[6]

3. Defend and Reform Democratic Institutions

Institutions can't defend themselves: people like you and me must defend our institutions. And to be worth defending, those institutions must *serve* the people.

For Americans, this means

- Organizing to protect voting rights at both state and federal levels

- Strengthening anti-corruption measures across all branches of government

- Modernizing the Electoral Count Act to prevent future attempts to overturn elections

- Rebalancing power between branches to limit executive overreach

As Justice Louis Brandeis wrote, "If we would guide by the light of reason, we must let our minds be bold."[7]

4. Practice Strategic Nonviolence

Nonviolent resistance isn't just morally superior to violence, it's also more effective: just ask the followers of Jesus, Mahatma Gandhi, or Dr. Martin Luther King Jr. Research by political scientists Erica Chenoweth and Maria Stephan has proven that nonviolent campaigns are more than *twice* as likely to succeed as violent ones.[8]

Nonviolent resistance works because it

- Allows broader participation across demographic groups

- Makes it harder for authorities to justify repression

- Causes security forces to question their loyalty to the regime

- Generates greater international support

- Builds stronger democratic foundations for the future

And don't misunderstand: nonviolence doesn't call for passive acceptance of authoritarian actions; far from it. Strategic nonviolence includes strikes, boycotts, mass demonstrations, disruption of normal life, direct confrontations with authority figures like ICE, and other forms of direct action that impose real costs on authoritarian regimes.

As civil rights leader Bayard Rustin observed, "The only weapon we have is our bodies, and we need to tuck them in places so wheels don't turn."[9]

5. Build Alternative Power Structures

Successful resistance movements don't just protest; they demonstrate the future by building better models of governance and making communities more resilient against authoritarian control.

For Americans facing incipient fascism, this means

- Strengthening local groups that directly address community needs

- Building worker cooperatives that model small-d democratic economics

- Creating community media including websites, podcasts, and low-power FM stations that provide reliable local information

- Participating in local government in ways that increase participation and transparency

- Supporting faith communities and civic organizations that become local centers and thus foster social cohesion

- Fielding a "shadow cabinet" filled with Democrats and Republicans who are committed to democracy and positive governance

These structures serve two crucial functions: they meet immediate needs, making resistance sustainable, and they prefigure the democratic society we're fighting to both preserve and create.

6. Engage Internationally

Authoritarianism is both an ancient and a global phenomenon, which is why resistance movements must be global as well. Successful efforts build international connections that provide support, resources, and can offer protection or even places to flee if necessary.

For Americans, international engagement means

- Building solidarity with democracy movements worldwide

- Learning from successful resistance strategies throughout history and in other countries

- Creating transnational efforts to regulate global platforms like social media

- Supporting international institutions that uphold democratic norms, from the UN to the International Criminal Court

The United States has often positioned itself as democracy's defender across the world. Now, ironically, Americans need to learn from democratic defenders in our own history and elsewhere.

7. Prepare for the Long Struggle

One of the most important lessons from successful resistance movements throughout history is that defeating authoritarianism is not a one-off, single-event victory but a long-term process requiring sustained sacrifice and persistence.

South Africa's anti-apartheid struggle lasted decades. Poland's Solidarity movement faced years of setbacks, including martial law, before achieving democracy. Chilean resistance to Pinochet suffered seventeen years of brutal repression before his removal.

Now that Trump and his allies are entrenched in our governmental, political, media, and economic systems, Americans must prepare for a marathon, not a sprint. This means

- Developing sustainable activism practices and communities that prevent burnout

- Creating intergenerational movements that pass knowledge to younger activists

- Building infrastructure for long-term organizing beyond election cycles

- Celebrating small victories to maintain morale during difficult periods

- Articulating a positive vision that sustains hope through dark times

As Czech dissident Václav Havel wrote during his country's darkest period: "Hope is not the conviction that something will turn out well, but the certainty that something makes sense, regardless of how it turns out."[10]

Reform: It Wasn't Just Trump— It Was the System That Fed Him

Donald Trump didn't emerge from a vacuum. He's the product of systems— corrupt, corroded, and increasingly anti-democratic, yes, but systems nonetheless—that made his rise not just possible but inevitable. If we only focus on removing Trump without addressing the deep corruption of Citizens United and other events and systems that produced him, we're simply setting the stage for the next authoritarian, who may be smarter, more disciplined, and ultimately more dangerous.

As a result, the deep question that our media almost never mentions is this: can democracy survive when it's for sale?

Our campaign finance system has effectively legalized bribery through the Supreme Court's disastrous all-Republican-appointee 5–4 Citizens United decision, which unleashed unlimited corporate and billionaire spending in lobbying and across our elections. As Justice John Paul Stevens warned in his dissent, the court's ruling "threatens to undermine the integrity of elected institutions across the Nation."[11] That prophecy came true with frightening speed as, post-2010, campaign spending exploded.

Billionaires have pumped fortunes into creating an infrastructure that supports authoritarianism, from think tanks that draft corporate-friendly policies, to well-paid media stars and outlets that spread lies and disinformation, to dark money groups that fund right-wing extremist candidates and initiatives.[12] These oligarchs and their corporations aren't investing out of patriotism (although that's always their claim); they expect returns in the form of tax cuts, deregulation, and policies that increase their wealth and power while attacking dissent and gutting the power of government, workers, and unions.

The result is a political system that only responds to the GOP's donor class and is openly hostile to the needs of ordinary Americans. As researchers Martin Gilens and Benjamin Page demonstrated in their landmark study, "economic elites and organized groups representing business interests have substantial independent impacts on U.S. government policy, while average citizens and mass-based interest groups have little or no independent influence."[13]

I've been running a contest on my radio show for twenty-two years: the winner will identify any one piece of legislation since the 1980 Reagan Revolution that was written by Republicans, passed Congress with a majority of Republican votes, and was signed into law by a Republican president that primarily benefits average working people or the poor instead of corporations or the rich. Nobody has ever won the autographed book I'm offering as a prize.

This system of legalized corruption reaches far beyond mere campaign contributions (although it's massive there). The revolving door between government and industry lets legislators and bureaucrats who write regulations "fail upward" to extremely well-paid jobs in the industries they once regulated. The growth of this Supreme Court–certified lobbying industry—which now spends over $3.7 billion annually—guarantees that corporate interests are dominant in every policy debate, while people advocating for the public interest are vastly outgunned.[14]

Media consolidation has compounded these problems. In 1983, fifty companies controlled most of America's media outlets. Today, just six corporations—several explicitly right-leaning—control 90 percent of what Americans see, hear, and read.[15] This concentration hasn't just kneecapped journalistic independence; it's invented "news" designed to maximize profit rather than inform citizens. The result is that facts have become optional, conspiracy theories flourish, and outrage drives decisions made in media boardrooms and editorial production meetings.

Our judiciary, meant by the Framers as, in part, a check on the president's political power, has instead become a partisan weapon. The billionaire- and corporate-funded Federalist Society has transformed a good number of our federal courts into bastions of pro-corporate, anti-worker jurisprudence. Right-wing judges have gutted voting rights, stripped us of labor protections, and shielded the morbidly rich from accountability, all while spouting bogus, pious claims that they're merely "originalists" and simply mind-reading the Framers—who were as disparate a group as any you could find today—as they pretend to "interpret" the Constitution.[16]

When Trump nominated Neil Gorsuch, Brett Kavanaugh, and Amy Coney Barrett to the Supreme Court, he wasn't just making routine appointments like most presidents before him who depended on the American Bar Association for guidance; instead, he and Mitch McConnell were completing a decades-long project to capture our nation's judiciary on behalf of corporations, the rich, and the ideologues of the authoritarian right. These aren't Trump's judges, as they'll long outlive him; they are, instead—since Trump stopped giving the ABA advance notice of nominations in 2017—the billionaire-funded Federalist Society's judges, vetted and approved by the same dark money networks that have systematically dismantled so many of our democratic guardrails.[17]

Reforming this system isn't about winning the next election; it's about ending our drift toward fascism and returning to the democratic principles laid out in the Declaration of Independence and the Constitution. This work we're undertaking requires undoing years of democratic backsliding with fundamental structural changes to revive our democracy. We must

- Overturn Citizens United through constitutional amendment or court reform (or both), ending the fiction that money equals speech and corporations have the same Constitutional rights as people.

- Implement public financing of elections to ensure candidates respond to voters, not donors. Seattle's "democracy voucher" program offers a promising model, where each voter receives four vouchers worth twenty-five dollars each that they can donate to candidates who agree to lower contribution limits.[18]

- Break up media monopolies to restore the vibrant, diverse, and independent press that we once enjoyed and democracy requires. In particular, the Telecommunications Act of 1996, which enabled massive media consolidation and let social media sites turn into unregulated propaganda mills, must be replaced with legislation that promotes local ownership, social media responsibility, and journalistic independence.[19]

- Require algorithmic transparency in social media by reforming or killing off Section 230 of the Telecommunications Act so people can see for themselves exactly how they're being influenced and by whom.

- Reform the Supreme Court through term limits, enforceable ethical standards, and potentially expansion, restoring its role as a neutral arbiter rather than a partisan weapon.

- Strengthen anti-corruption laws to close the revolving door between government and industry while limiting the influence of big, dark money in lobbying.

These reforms aren't partisan. They're pro-democracy. And they're essential if we want to prevent the next Trump, who will almost certainly be far more effective at dismantling our democratic institutions than Donald, JD, and Elon have been.

The choice before us isn't between left and right but between democracy and authoritarianism. As the famous conservative Judge J. Michael Luttig recently warned, "America is at war with itself over our democracy" and facing "the most perilous moment for our democracy since the founding of the United States."[20]

Democracy can't survive when it's for sale to the highest bidder. These reforms aren't optional; they're existential.

The AI Authoritarian Threat

Pope Leo XIV labeled AI one of the main threats facing humanity, saying it poses challenges to human dignity, justice, and labor.[21] He's right, but it's even worse than that; AI represents, unless it's rigorously regulated, a threat to democracy itself.

In every generation, the enemies of democracy change costumes, nations, and languages, but their playbook remains eerily familiar. They lie, divide, intimidate, and exploit every available tool to consolidate power. In the 1930s they used newspapers and radio, in the 2010s it was social media, and now, in 2025, the newest and most dangerous weapon in the authoritarian arsenal is artificial intelligence.

Make no mistake: AI isn't just another "new technology." It's power, scaled. And in the hands of the hard right that is trying to end our republican form of government, it has the potential to become the most effective tool for dismantling democracy ever invented.[22]

Authoritarians—whether MAGA-aligned in the United States or

part of the global movement that includes Putin, Orbán, Modi, MBS, and others—are not blind to the potential of AI. They understand it instinctively: its ability to pretend to be human, to deceive, to surveil, and to dominate. While progressives and democratic institutions are scrambling to get a handle on its implications, authoritarians in America, Russia, and around the world have already started weaponizing it with devastating efficiency.

A single AI machine can now generate *millions of personalized political messages* in seconds, each calibrated to manipulate voters' specific fears or biases. It can (and currently is being used to) create entire fake news outlets, populate them with AI-generated journalists, and flood your social feed or web search with content that looks real, sounds real, and feels familiar, all without a single human behind it. Imagine the power of Joseph Goebbels's propaganda machine, but with superintelligence behind the wheel and zero friction. That's where we're heading in the 2028 presidential election.

And that's just the beginning.

Authoritarian regimes can—and already are—using AI to surveil and intimidate their citizens. What China has perfected with facial recognition, social media, and loyalty scoring, MAGA-aligned figures in the United States are rushing to adopt and adapt. Right-wing sheriffs and local governments could soon use AI to track protesters, compile digital dossiers, and "predict" criminal behavior in communities deemed politically undesirable. If the government knows not just where you are, but what you're thinking, organizing, or reading—and it can fabricate "evidence" to match—freedom of thought (much less freedom of expression) becomes a quaint memory.

This isn't theoretical. In 2024, Republicans deployed AI-generated robocalls impersonating Joe Biden telling voters to stay home, and millions did. In the next cycle, it's safe to predict that we'll see entire portions of election campaigns waged by AI bots masquerading as voters, influencers, news media, and even public officials.

The goal here for the hard right that doesn't embrace democracy but wants America to become an authoritarian state isn't just to win; it's to delegitimize the democratic process itself as Orbán and Putin have done. Because once trust is broken—once people believe that "both sides lie" or that "you can't believe anything anymore"—then, inevitably (history tells us), strongmen step into the void with promises of order, purity, and salvation.

And when they do, AI will also be there to help them enforce the new "order" in their "orderly society" where dissent has become a crime and fear of speaking out stalks the land.

Imagine a future where police departments outsource their decision-making to "neutral" algorithms, algorithms coded with the biases of their creators, like Musk is doing by training his Grok AI on X. Where AI-driven court systems deny permits, benefits, or even due process based on *Majority Report*-style "behavioral profiles." Where (like in China today) loyalty to the regime is rewarded with access, and dissent is flagged by invisible systems you can't appeal or even know about for sure.

That's not democracy. That's techno-feudalism, wrapped in a red-white-and-blue flag.

If we allow the billionaires who fund the hard right to continue merging political power with unregulated AI, we *will* see the rise of a system where freedom is algorithmically rationed.

Elections will still happen, of course, but outcomes will be predetermined without our even realizing it. Dissent will still exist, but only in controlled pockets, and it'll be easy to monitor and suppress through harassment, intimidation, and arrest. History books will be written, edited, and distributed by AI code optimized to tell the oligarch's story while suppressing the true stories of America (particularly those of racial and gender minorities). In this Brave New America, the "news" will be whatever the regime's AI decides you should see.

This is not science fiction. It is the logical endpoint of unregulated, authoritarian-aligned artificial intelligence in the hands of unaccountable billionaires and despotic governments.

So what can we do?

To start, we must treat the regulation of AI and the people who own/use/deploy it as a democratic survival issue. That means

- Banning the use of deepfakes in political ads

- Enforcing transparency on algorithmic decision-making

- Creating public, open-source alternatives to corporate-controlled models

- Creating disinformation-catching infrastructure as we would biological or nuclear weapons (that are also not just dangerous, but potentially civilization-ending)

- Demanding that social media outlets publish their algorithms so we can see how we're being manipulated

And we must do it now.

Because history teaches us that once authoritarianism takes root, it rarely gives up power voluntarily. Particularly when (like with the innovations of the nineteenth and twentieth centuries) it has new tools that are more powerful than those who would protest and try to defend democracy. The longer we wait, the more embedded, autonomous, and intelligent these systems will become, and the more wealth and power their owners will accumulate. We're not just fighting bad actors anymore; we're fighting machines trained by them to think and behave like them.

The battle for democracy in the age of AI won't be won with slogans or optimism alone. It will take law, oversight, courage, and above all, vigilance. I end every radio show with "democracy is not a spectator sport." If we want to preserve the sacred right of self-governance we inherited from previous generations, we have no choice but to immediately recognize the existential threat in front of us and act with appropriate urgency.

This time, the fight isn't just against the usual suspects.

This time, the algorithm is watching.

Remember: The Cost of Forgetting

History shows us that societies that fail to honestly confront (and teach their children about) their darkest chapters are, more often than not, doomed to repeat them. Germany's unflinching confrontation with its Nazi past—through education, memorials, and legal accountability—stands in stark contrast to Japan's reluctance to fully acknowledge its wartime atrocities, or to America's halting efforts to address our legacy of slavery (and the ongoing "Lost Cause" Confederate mythos) as well as the (ongoing) genocide against this continent's Indigenous peoples.

The consequences of this collective amnesia are all around us, from the Confederate flags on January 6th to the new efforts to strip science and history from our schools. When we fail to teach children about the horrors of the Holocaust, for example, anti-Semitism resurges. When we allow Confederate monuments to stand unchallenged, white nationalism finds fertile ground. When we call January 6th "legitimate political discourse" (as multiple Republican elected officials have done) rather than the attempted coup that it was, we prepare the soil for the next, potentially successful insurrection.

Memory is not passive; it's an active, ongoing process, because it's the foundation of our present and shapes our future. As philosopher George Santayana famously noted, "Those who cannot remember the past are condemned to repeat it."[23] But just remembering isn't enough: we must draw the right lessons, form the true conclusions, and pass along the honest truths to our children from history.

The most dangerous form of forgetting isn't complete amnesia, it's sanitization, where historical atrocities are stripped of their horror and repackaged as noble struggles (as is being done today and has been done for over a century around the Civil War) or unfortunate mistakes (like the way we deal with the lies that led us into Vietnam, Iraq, and Afghanistan). We see this in "conservative" attempts to rebrand the Confederacy as a fight for "states' rights" rather than to preserve slavery, or in textbooks, stories, and even movies and TV shows (remember the westerns of the mid-twentieth century?) that minimize the genocide of Native Americans as an "unfortunate" consequence of "westward expansion."

I remember well back in the 1980s when we'd moved to Atlanta from New Hampshire, our first time living in the South. Over dinner one night I asked our son, then in public elementary school, what he'd studied in school that day. "We learned about the War of Northern Aggression," he told Louise and me to our slack-jawed amazement.

This selective amnesia and its promotion across our nation's social and political culture isn't accidental. It's a deliberate strategy by the beneficiaries of white supremacy and genocide to avoid accountability and perpetuate the systems that help them retain their own power. As journalist Jelani Cobb notes, "When we speak of history, we're not speaking about what happened in the past. We're talking about who has the power to define what happened."[24]

Authoritarian movements understand this power all too well. Their first target is almost always historical truth, banning books, removing "uncomfortable" topics from school curricula, and attacking archives and academic freedom. The world saw it in Germany, Spain, Italy, and Japan in the run-up to World War II, and is seeing it now in Russia, Hungary, and—tragically—here in the United States. They know that controlling the past is essential to controlling the future. As Hitler wrote in Chapter 10 of *Mein Kampf*, "The victor will never be asked if he told the truth," and as he later said in a 1935 speech at the Reichsparteitag, "He alone, who owns the youth, also seizes the future."

Resisting this erasure requires commitment to what I learned when I lived there in the 1980s, what modern-day Germans call *Erinnerungskultur*: a "culture of remembrance" that actively preserves memory of historical crimes and treats them not as ancient history but as living warnings. This includes

- Creating and preserving memorials to historical atrocities

- Supporting honest education about our darkest chapters

- Recording and amplifying the testimonies of survivors and witnesses

- Establishing truth and reconciliation processes

- Holding perpetrators accountable regardless of time elapsed

As Holocaust survivor Elie Wiesel reminded us, "For the dead and the living, we must bear witness."[25] And we must bear that witness not to wallow in guilt, but to make absolutely sure that "never again" is a lived reality instead of just an empty slogan.

The American experiment has always been, at multiple levels, a contradiction: founded on principles of freedom while practicing slavery, promising equality while enforcing segregation, celebrating democracy while denying the vote to millions. But what has kept our American experiment—the first in the history of the civilized world—alive is our willingness, however halting and imperfect, to confront these contradictions and nonetheless (or even because of them) strive toward that more perfect union that our Constitution's preamble promises.

Hope Is a Discipline

In dark times, hope isn't a passive emotion: it's a discipline, a practice we must cultivate daily through action and solidarity, a discipline that keeps us moving forward no matter how hard things get. It keeps us grounded and focused on a positive future.

Mariame Kaba, the prison abolitionist and organizer, puts it perfectly: "Hope doesn't preclude feeling sadness or frustration or anger or any other emotion that makes total sense. Hope isn't an emotion, you know? Hope is not optimism. Hope is a discipline. . . . we have to practice it every single day."[26]

Given that the enemies of democracy and advocates of authoritarianism are massively well-funded, have been liberated by Republicans on the Supreme Court, and control a large part of our media and social media infrastructure, the path forward won't be easy. There will be setbacks, moments of despair, and very real dangers. But if history tells us anything, it's that people facing far worse odds have repeatedly and successfully defended or even brought into being (as our Founders did) democracy against authoritarian threats. If South Koreans could defend their democracy against corruption, if Chileans could end Pinochet's brutal regime, if South Africans could dismantle apartheid, if America could prevail against the fascists of the Confederacy, then we modern Americans can certainly protect our democratic institutions.

In the famous words of anthropologist Margaret Mead: "Never doubt that a small group of thoughtful, committed citizens can change the world; indeed, it's the only thing that ever has."

The question isn't whether we can defeat authoritarianism: history both proves that we repeatedly have and that, going forward, we can. The question is whether we will, like our forebearers, again muster the courage, wisdom, and solidarity to do so.

Democracy isn't just a system of government: it's a moral commitment to human dignity, equality, and freedom handed down to us by

Indigenous people (as I detail in *The Hidden History of American Democracy*), preserved by generations of Americans willing to fight and die for it. Its defense isn't just political; it's profoundly personal and the work that today falls to you and me. Thus, each of us must decide what role we'll play in this defining struggle of our time.

As you close this book, I hope you'll carry not just an understanding of the threat we face, but a deepened commitment to the values of democracy that are so worth fighting for, along with a renewed and practical knowledge of how to join that fight effectively.

The future isn't yet written. It's created, day by day, via our collective choices. This is why it's so imperative that each of us make choices that our grandchildren will thank us for.

The billionaire authoritarians and their toadies believe their hour has come. Let's prove them wrong.

Epilogue

*If destruction be our lot, we must ourselves be its author and
finisher. As a nation of freemen, we must live through all time,
or die by suicide.* —Abraham Lincoln, Lyceum Address, 1838

Trump isn't the first Republican president to have seized the
White House by fraud. In fact, the historical pattern is far more disturbing:
every Republican president since Eisenhower has either directly stolen the
presidency or inherited their position from someone who did.

Nixon started this treasonous tradition in 1968. While President
Johnson was desperately working to end the Vietnam War, Nixon secretly
sent envoys to persuade South Vietnamese leaders to boycott peace talks,
promising them better terms after his election. Johnson discovered this
sabotage when the FBI brought him the wiretaps; he confronted Nixon
directly, calling it what it was: "This is treason."[1] Nixon's scheme worked,
however, prolonging the war that killed an additional 22,000 Americans
and over a million Vietnamese. And Johnson took this crime to his grave;
his library didn't release the tapes for decades.

The pattern continued with Reagan in the election of 1980. As
recently confirmed by former Texas House Speaker Ben Barnes, Reagan's
campaign struck a deal with Iran's Ayatollah Khomeini to keep fifty-two
American hostages captive until after the election, deliberately sabotag-
ing President Carter's negotiations for their release.[2] The hostages were
freed the very minute Reagan was sworn in, and his administration later
secretly sold weapons to Iran (leading to the Iran-Contra scandal), thus
keeping his corrupt bargain.

George H. W. Bush leveraged Reagan's illegitimate presidency to get
into the White House himself, and then used Attorney General Bill Barr
to shut down the Iran-Contra investigation by pardoning six key figures
before they could implicate him.[3]

The Supreme Court handed George W. Bush the presidency in 2000
by halting Florida's recount, despite Gore winning the popular vote by

163

over 500,000 ballots. A later investigation by major newspapers confirmed Gore would have won Florida under any fair counting standard.[4] And let's not forget that Bush's brother, Florida Governor Jeb Bush, purged at least 57,000 mostly Black voters from the rolls just months before the election that was "decided" by fewer than 600 votes.[5]

Trump continued this tradition in 2016, benefiting from voter suppression orchestrated by Republican secretaries of state and Kris Kobach's Interstate Crosscheck program that purged millions of legitimate voters—mostly people of color—from the rolls.[6] He also benefited from Russian interference through social media manipulation, as documented by Robert Mueller's investigation.[7]

Finally, Trump's payment to silence Stormy Daniels—the crime that Manhattan DA Alvin Bragg successfully prosecuted, leading to Trump's thirty-four felony convictions for election fraud—was crucial to keeping Trump's candidacy afloat after the "grab 'em by the pussy" scandal. Without those illegal payoffs violating campaign finance laws and keeping the Stormy Daniels and Karen McDougal stories under wraps, Trump almost certainly would have lost to Hillary Clinton.

America has ignored GOP crimes to seize the White House for far too long. Ford's pardon of Nixon set a destructive precedent of presidential immunity that has echoed through decades, leading to packed courts, unnecessary wars, massive tax cuts for billionaires, and the gutting of America's middle class.

And now it's been amplified by six Republicans on the Supreme Court ruling that Trump can commit crimes while in office with relative impunity, an immunity that he's apparently reveling in.

It's time to break this pattern and finally hold at least one (convicted) criminal Republican president accountable.

Notes

Introduction

1   U.S. House of Representatives, Select Committee to Investigate the January 6th Attack on the United States Capitol, Final Report, (Washington, DC: U.S. Government Publishing Office, 2022), https://www.govinfo.gov/app/details/GPO-J6 -REPORT.

2   Peter Baker, "A Mob and the Breach of Democracy: The Violent End of the Trump Era," *New York Times*, January 6, 2021, https://www.nytimes.com/2021/01/06/us/poli tics/trump-congress.html.

3   Ibid.

4   FBI Washington Field Office, "Video and Additional Information Released Regarding January 5 Pipe Bomb Investigation," FBI.gov, September 8, 2021, https://www.fbi .gov/contact-us/field-offices/washingtondc/news/press-releases/fbi-washing ton-field-office-releases-video-and-additional-information-regarding-the-pipe -bomb-investigation-090821.

5   Select Committee to Investigate the January 6th Attack on the United States Capitol, *The January 6th Report*, foreword by David Remnick and epilogue by Jamie Raskin (Celadon Books, 2022).

6   "MAGA Movement," *Encyclopædia Britannica*, accessed May 8, 2025, https://www.bri tannica.com/topic/MAGA-movement.

7   Donald J. Trump, "Address Accepting the Presidential Nomination at the Republican National Convention in Cleveland, Ohio," The American Presidency Project, University of California, Santa Barbara, July 21, 2016, https://www.presidency.ucsb .edu/documents/address-accepting-the-presidential-nomination-the-republican -national-convention-cleveland.

8   Glenn Kessler, "President Trump's False Claims of Vote Fraud: A Chronology," *Washington Post*, November 5, 2020, https://www.washingtonpost.com/politics/2020/11/05 /president-trumps-false-claims-vote-fraud-chronology/.

9   Timothy Snyder, "The American Abyss." *New York Times Magazine*, January 9, 2021, https://www.nytimes.com/2021/01/09/magazine/trump-coup.html.

10   Stephan Malinowski, "Hitler's Wealthy Backers: How German Elite Facilitated the Nazi Rise," HistoryExtra, *BBC History Magazine*, November 8, 2018, https:// www.historyextra.com/period/second-world-war/hitler-millionaire-backers-how -elite-facilitated-rise-nazis-third-reich/.

11   "Venezuela: Chávez Allies Pack Supreme Court," Human Rights Watch, December 13, 2004, https://www.hrw.org/news/2004/12/13/venezuela-chavez-allies-pack -supreme-court.

12   Rob Schmitz, "Hungary's Orban Demonstrates How to Dismantle Democracy," NPR, April 20, 2025, https://www.npr.org/2025/04/20/nx-s1-5338596/hungary -viktor-orban-democracy.

13   Andrew Marantz, "Does Hungary Offer a Glimpse of Our Authoritarian Future?" *New Yorker*, July 4, 2022, https://www.newyorker.com/magazine/2022/07/04/does -hungary-offer-a-glimpse-of-our-authoritarian-future.

14 Michael D'Antonio, "The Men Who Gave Trump His Brutal Worldview," *Politico Magazine*, March 29, 2016, https://www.politico.com/magazine/story/2016/03/2016-donald-trump-brutal-worldview-father-coach-213750.

15 Jim Zirin, "The Man Who First Fueled Donald Trump's Paranoid Politics," *Time*, April 14, 2017, https://time.com/4690261/donald-trump-paranoid/.

16 Tom Nichols, "The GOP's Ongoing Moral Surrender to Trump," *The Atlantic*, January 29, 2024, https://www.theatlantic.com/newsletters/archive/2024/01/the-gops-ongoing-moral-surrender-to-trump/677286/.

17 Peter Stone, "Trump's Picks to Reward Top Donors Who Helped Him Win, Watchdogs Say," *The Guardian*, November 26, 2024, https://www.theguardian.com/us-news/2024/nov/26/trump-administration-loyalists-donors.

18 Thomas E. Patterson, "News Coverage of the 2016 Presidential Campaign," Shorenstein Center on Media, Politics and Public Policy, Harvard Kennedy School. September 2016, https://shorensteincenter.org/news-coverage-2016-general-election/.

19 Sidney Blumenthal, "Trump Once Seemed Invincible. Then Kamala Harris Broke the Spell," *The Guardian*, August 6, 2024, https://www.theguardian.com/commentisfree/article/2024/aug/06/trump-kamala-harris-presidential-election.

20 Amy Gardner, "Election Workers Describe 'Hateful' Threats after Trump's False Claims," *Washington Post*, June 21, 2022, https://www.washingtonpost.com/national-security/2022/06/21/ruby-freeman-shaye-moss-jan6-testimony/.

21 Rob Stein, "Fauci Reveals He Has Received Death Threats and His Daughters Have Been Harassed," NPR, August 5, 2020, https://www.npr.org/sections/coronavirus-live-updates/2020/08/05/899415906/fauci-reveals-he-has-received-death-threats-and-his-daughters-have-been-harassed.

22 Elizabeth Shogren, "Scientist Who Resisted Censorship of Climate Report Lost Her Job," *Canada's National Observer*, February 16, 2019, https://www.nationalobserver.com/2019/02/16/news/scientist-who-resisted-censorship-climate-report-lost-her-job.

23 John Nichols, "Four Years after 'Citizens United,' There Is Real Movement to Remove Big Money from Politics," *The Nation*, January 21, 2014, https://www.thenation.com/article/archive/four-years-after-citizens-united-there-real-movement-remove-big-money-politics/.

24 Ezra Klein, "Donald Trump's Success Reveals a Frightening Weakness in American Democracy," *Vox*, November 7, 2016, https://www.vox.com/policy-and-politics/2016/11/7/13532178/donald-trump-american-democracy-weakness.

25 Linda Greenhouse, "The Supreme Court We Need," *New York Review of Books*, November 5, 2020, https://www.nybooks.com/articles/2020/11/05/the-supreme-court-we-need/.

26 Lilie Chouliaraki and Kathryn Claire Higgins, "Trump Rode Pain and Victimhood to Power, but Grievance May Not Be an Effective Basis for Governing," LSE USAPP (blog), January 22, 2025, https://blogs.lse.ac.uk/usappblog/2025/01/22/trump-rode-pain-and-victimhood-to-power-but-grievance-may-not-be-a-effective-basis-for-governing/.

27 Jane Mayer, "The Reclusive Hedge-Fund Tycoon behind the Trump Presidency," *New Yorker*, March 27, 2017, https://www.newyorker.com/magazine/2017/03/27/the-reclusive-hedge-fund-tycoon-behind-the-trump-presidency.

28 The Guardian Editorial Board, "The Guardian View on Donald Trump's Power Grab: A Coup Veiled by Chaos," *The Guardian*, February 3, 2025, https://www.theguardian.com/commentisfree/2025/feb/03/the-guardian-view-on-donald-trumps-power-grab-a-coup-veiled-by-chaos.

29 Jason Stanley, "The End of US Democracy Was All Too Predictable," Project Syndicate, November 6, 2024, https://www.project-syndicate.org/commentary /trump-election-inequality-meant-that-us-democracy-was-doomed-by-jason -stanley-2024-11.

30 Jennifer Rubin, "Republicans Should Have Booted Trump Long before He Threatened the Constitution," Washington Post, December 5, 2022, https://www.washing tonpost.com/opinions/2022/12/05/rubin-trump-constitution-threat-gop/.

CHAPTER 1

1   Keeanga-Yamahtta Taylor, "The Bitter Fruits of Trump's White-Power Presidency," New Yorker, January 12, 2021, https://www.newyorker.com/news/our-columnists /the-bitter-fruits-of-trumps-white-power-presidency.

2   Oliver Laughland, "Donald Trump and the Central Park Five: The Racially Charged Rise of a Demagogue," The Guardian, February 17, 2016, https://www.theguardian .com/us-news/2016/feb/17/central-park-five-donald-trump-jogger-rape-case-new -york.

3   Katie Warren, "I Visited Trump's Childhood Neighborhood on the Outskirts of NYC, and It Didn't Take Long to See Why He's Called It an 'Oasis,'" Business Insider, November 19, 2018, https://www.businessinsider.com/donald-trump-child hood-neighborhood-queens-new-york-city-photos-2018-11.

4   Alice Cattley, "The Story of Fred Trump: How Donald Trump's Father Made His Millions," LoveMoney, February 9, 2024, https://www.lovemoney.com/galleries /138315/the-story-of-fred-trump-how-donald-trumps-father-made-his-millions.

5   Peter Dreier, "Trump's Housing Hypocrisy," The American Prospect, March 10, 2017, https://prospect.org/economy/trump-s-housing-hypocrisy/.

6   Patti Davis, "Fred Trump Tells You Everything There Is to Know about Donald," Daily Beast, August 4, 2020, https://www.thedailybeast.com/fred-trump-tells-you -everything-there-is-to-know-about-donald.

7   Martin Pengelly, "Donald Trump's Behavior Was Shaped by His 'Sociopath' Father, Niece Writes in Bombshell Book," The Guardian, July 7, 2020, https://www.theguard ian.com/us-news/2020/jul/07/donald-trump-abuse-father-niece-mary-book.

8   Ibid.

9   Ibid.

10 Nina Burleigh, "How Donald Trump's Mother Did—and Didn't—Shape His Life," Vanity Fair, May 7, 2020, https://www.vanityfair.com/style/2020/05/the-mystery-of -donald-trumps-mother.

11 Ibid.

12 Pengelly, "Donald Trump's Behavior Was Shaped by His 'Sociopath' Father."

13 Marie Brenner, "After the Gold Rush," Vanity Fair, September 1990, https://www.vanity fair.com/magazine/2015/07/donald-ivana-trump-divorce-prenup-marie-brenner.

14 Michael Kranish, "Trump Pressured His Alcoholic Brother about His Career. Now He Has Regrets," Washington Post, August 8, 2019, https://www.washingtonpost.com /politics/trump-pressured-his-alcoholic-brother-about-his-career-now-he-has -regrets-/2019/08/07/58ec2d70-b216-11e9-8f6c-7828e68cb15f_story.html.

15 Michael Kruse, "'Weakness Was the Greatest Sin of All': How a Lifelong Need to Seem Strong Made Trump Vulnerable," Politico Magazine, October 2, 2020, https:// www.politico.com/news/magazine/2020/10/02/trump-weakness-covid-425323.

16 Brenner, "After the Gold Rush."

17 U.S. Department of Justice, United States v. Fred C. Trump, Donald Trump, and Trump Management, Inc., Case No. 73–1529 (E.D.N.Y. 1973), Civil Rights Litigation Clearinghouse, https://clearinghouse.net/case/15342/

18 Michael Kranish and Marc Fisher, "Inside the Government's Racial Bias Case against Donald Trump's Company, and How He Fought It," *Washington Post*, January 23, 2016, https://www.washingtonpost.com/politics/inside-the-governments -racial-bias-case-against-donald-trumps-company-and-how-he-fought-it/2016 /01/23/fb90163e-bfbe-11e5-bcda-62a36b394160_story.html.

19 Michael E. Miller, "50 Years Later, Disagreements over Young Trump's Military Academy Record," *Washington Post*, January 9, 2016, https://www.washingtonpost .com/politics/decades-later-disagreement-over-young-trumps-military-academy -post/2016/01/09/907a67b2-b3e0-11e5-a842-0feb51d1d124_story.html.

20 Patrice Taddonio, "Trump the 'Bully': How Childhood and Military School Shaped the Future President," *PBS Frontline*, September 22, 2020, https://www.pbs.org/wgbh /frontline/article/trump-the-bully-how-childhood-military-school-shaped-the-fu ture-president/.

21 Miller, "50 Years Later, Disagreements over Young Trump's Military Academy Record."

22 Kranish and Fisher, "Inside the Government's Racial Bias Case against Donald Trump's Company, and How He Fought It."

23 David Rothkopf, "Can Wharton Revoke Trump's Economics Degree Now?" *Daily Beast*, January 8, 2021. https://www.thedailybeast.com/can-wharton-revoke-trumps -economics-degree-now/.

24 Andrea Bernstein, "'American Oligarchs' Reveals How Trump, Kushner Families Learned to Work the System," NPR, January 8, 2020, https://www.npr.org/2020 /01/08/794509417/american-oligarchs-reveals-how-trump-kushner-families -learned-to-work-the-system.

25 Emily Badger, "How Donald Trump Abandoned His Father's Middle-Class Housing Empire for Luxury Building," *Washington Post*, August 10, 2015, https://www .washingtonpost.com/news/wonk/wp/2015/08/10/the-middle-class-housing -empire-donald-trump-abandoned-for-luxury-building/.

26 David Barstow, Susanne Craig, and Russ Buettner, "Trump Engaged in Suspect Tax Schemes as He Reaped Riches from His Father," *New York Times*, October 2, 2018, https://www.nytimes.com/interactive/2018/10/02/us/politics/donald-trump -tax-schemes-fred-trump.html.

27 Ibid.

28 Jane Mayer, "Donald Trump's Ghostwriter Tells All," *New Yorker*, July 25, 2016, https://www.newyorker.com/magazine/2016/07/25/donald-trumps-ghostwriter -tells-all.

29 Ibid.

30 Ibid.

31 Ann E. Marimow, "Chief Justice Says Courts Must Be Free to Check 'Excesses' of Congress, White House," *Washington Post*, May 8, 2025, https://www.washington post.com/politics/2025/05/07/chief-justice-roberts-judicial-independence -buffalo/.

32 Axios Staff, "Call Notes Show Trump Urged DOJ to Declare Election 'Corrupt,'" Axios, July 30, 2021, https://www.axios.com/2021/07/30/trump-voter-fraud-doj -pressure.

33 Steve Peoples and Calvin Woodward, "Trump Claims 'Millions' Voted Illegally,

Without Evidence," *PBS NewsHour*, November 27, 2016, https://www.pbs.org/news hour/politics/trump-claims-millions-voted-illegally.

34 Philip Bump, "Trump Moves to Legally Enforce 2020 Election Denialism," *Washington Post*, April 10, 2025, https://www.washingtonpost.com/opinions/2025/04/10/trump-krebs-election-denialism/.

35 Michael D. Shear and Maggie Haberman, "Trump Defends Initial Remarks on Charlottesville; Again Blames 'Both Sides,'" *New York Times*, August 15, 2017, https://www.nytimes.com/2017/08/15/us/politics/trump-press-conference-char lottesville.html.

36 Maggie Haberman and Michael S. Schmidt, "Trump Gives Clemency to More Allies, Including Manafort, Stone and Charles Kushner," *New York Times*, December 23, 2020, https://www.nytimes.com/2020/12/23/us/politics/trump-pardon -manafort-stone.html.

37 Mary L. Trump, *Too Much and Never Enough: How My Family Created the World's Most Dangerous Man* (Simon & Schuster, 2020), 196–201.

38 Susan B. Glasser, "The World Shook as America Raged," *New Yorker*, January 8, 2021, https://www.newyorker.com/news/our-columnists/the-world-shook-as -america-raged.

CHAPTER 2

1 U.S. Department of Justice, United States v. Fred C. Trump, Donald Trump, and Trump Management, Inc., Case No. 73-1529, (E.D.N.Y. 1973); Wayne Barrett, *Trump: The Deals and the Downfall* (HarperCollins, 1992), 97–99.

2 Marie Brenner, "How Donald Trump and Roy Cohn's Ruthless Symbiosis Changed America," *Vanity Fair*, August 2017; Frank Rich, "The Original Donald Trump," *New York Magazine*, April 29, 2018.

3 Jonathan Mahler and Matt Flegenheimer, "What Donald Trump Learned From Roy Cohn," *New York Times*, June 20, 2016.

4 Nicholas von Hoffman, *Citizen Cohn: The Life and Times of Roy Cohn* (Double-day, 1988), 13–15; Sidney Zion, *The Autobiography of Roy Cohn* (Lyle Stuart, 1988), 22–25.

5 Zion, *The Autobiography of Roy Cohn*, 78–79; Michael Kruse, "The True Story of Donald Trump's First Campaign Speech—in 1987," *Politico Magazine*, February 5, 2016.

6 Robert and Michael Meeropol, *We Are Your Sons: The Legacy of Ethel and Julius Rosenberg* (University of Illinois Press, 1986), 48–52; Sam Roberts, "The Brother Who Sent Ethel Rosenberg to the Electric Chair," *New York Times*, September 14, 2015.

7 Sam Roberts, "A Decade Later, the Rosenberg File Is Still Open," *New York Times*, August 16, 1993; Sam Roberts, "Greenglass Changed His Story About Sister's Role," *New York Times*, October 8, 2008.

8 David M. Oshinsky, *A Conspiracy So Immense: The World of Joe McCarthy* (Oxford University Press, 2005), 188–195; Ellen Schrecker, *Many Are the Crimes: McCarthyism in America* (Princeton University Press, 1998), 142–148.

9 Thomas Doherty, *Cold War, Cool Medium: Television, McCarthyism, and American Culture* (Columbia University Press, 2003), 162–167; Oshinsky, *A Conspiracy So Immense*, 256–260.

10 Senate Committee on Government Operations, "Special Senate Investigation on Charges and Countercharges Involving: Secretary of the Army Robert T. Stevens,

John G. Adams, H. Struve Hensel and Senator Joe McCarthy, Roy M. Cohn, and Francis P. Carr," 83rd Congress, 1954.

11 von Hoffman, *Citizen Cohn*, 142–146; Gary Cartwright, "The Mob Comes to Wall Street," *Texas Monthly*, April 1992; Robert I. Friedman, "The Gangster's Cousin," *The Nation*, November 16, 1998.

12 James B. Stewart, "The Day Jeffrey Epstein Told Me He Had Dirt on Powerful People," *New York Times*, August 12, 2019; Timothy L. O'Brien, *TrumpNation: The Art of Being the Donald* (Warner Books, 2005), 125–130.

13 Ken Auletta, "Don't Mess with Roy Cohn," *Esquire*, December 1978, 41–43; Tom Robbins, "The Last Testament of Roy Cohn," *Village Voice*, April 27, 1988.

14 Donald Trump with Tony Schwartz, *The Art of the Deal* (Random House, 1987), 93–94; Brenner, "How Donald Trump and Roy Cohn's Ruthless Symbiosis Changed America."

15 Wayne Barrett, *Trump: The Deals and the Downfall* (HarperCollins, 1992), 97–99; Nikole Hannah-Jones, "Living Apart: How the Government Betrayed a Landmark Civil Rights Law," *ProPublica*, June 25, 2015.

16 Trump and Schwartz, *The Art of the Deal*, 96–97; Brenner, "How Donald Trump and Roy Cohn's Ruthless Symbiosis Changed America."

17 U.S. Department of Justice, United States v. Fred C. Trump, Donald Trump, and Trump Management, Inc., Case No. 73–1529, (E.D.N.Y. 1973); Barrett, *Trump: The Deals and the Downfall*, 97–99; Mahler and Flegenheimer, "What Donald Trump Learned From Roy Cohn."

18 Brenner, "How Donald Trump and Roy Cohn's Ruthless Symbiosis Changed America"; Rich, "The Original Donald Trump."

19 von Hoffman, *Citizen Cohn*, 328–332; Gwenda Blair, *The Trumps: Three Generations of Builders and a Presidential Candidate* (Simon & Schuster, 2015), 240–246.

20 Auletta, "Don't Mess with Roy Cohn," 46; Brenner, "How Donald Trump and Roy Cohn's Ruthless Symbiosis Changed America."

21 Auletta, "Don't Mess with Roy Cohn," 46; Barrett, *Trump: The Deals and the Downfall*, 115.

22 David A. Fahrenthold, "Trump Recorded Having Extremely Lewd Conversation about Women in 2005," *Washington Post*, October 8, 2016; Glenn Kessler, "Trump's False Claim That He 'Grabbed' the Access Hollywood Tape," *Washington Post*, November 29, 2017.

23 von Hoffman, *Citizen Cohn*, 194; Auletta, "Don't Mess with Roy Cohn," 47.

24 Maggie Haberman and Alexander Burns, "Donald Trump's Other Campaign Foe: The 'Lowest Form of Life' News Media," *New York Times*, August 12, 2016; Dan Barry and Serge F. Kovaleski, "Serge Kovaleski, Reporter Mocked by Trump: 'I Have No Idea What He Was Doing,'" *New York Times*, November 26, 2015.

25 "3,500 Lawsuits: Trump's Unprecedented Legal Troubles," *USA Today*, June 1, 2016; James D. Zirin, *Plaintiff in Chief: A Portrait of Donald Trump in 3,500 Lawsuits* (All Points Books, 2019), 12–24.

26 Auletta, "Don't Mess with Roy Cohn," 45–48; von Hoffman, *Citizen Cohn*, 214–220.

27 Jonathan Greenberg, "Trump Lied to Me about His Wealth to Get onto the Forbes 400. Here Are the Tapes," *Washington Post*, April 20, 2018; Joe Hagan, "How Donald Trump Beat the New York Times Like a Dog," *New York Magazine*, January 26, 2016.

28 Oshinsky, *A Conspiracy So Immense*, 310–315; Doherty, *Cold War, Cool Medium*, 172–178.

29 Katie Reilly, "Here Are All the Times Donald Trump Insulted Mexico," *Time*, August 31, 2016; Katie Reilly, "Donald Trump Calls for 'Complete Shutdown' of Muslim Entry to U.S.," *Time*, December 7, 2015; Julie Hirschfeld Davis and Maggie Haberman, "Trump Gives Credence to False Claim That Deep State Is Trying to Take Him Down," *New York Times*, August 10, 2018.

30 von Hoffman, *Citizen Cohn*, 328–332; Auletta, "Don't Mess with Roy Cohn," 47–48.

31 Michael S. Schmidt, "Comey: Trump Asked for 'Loyalty,' Wanted Him to 'Let' Flynn Investigation 'Go,'" NBC News, June 7, 2017; Josh Dawsey, "Trump Blasts Sessions: 'VERY Weak' on Clinton Emails," *Politico*, July 25, 2017.

32 Wayne Barrett, "Donald Trump Wouldn't Have Existed without Roy Cohn," *Daily Beast*, January 24, 2019; Barrett, *Trump: The Deals and the Downfall*, 115–118.

33 Peter Baker and Neil Irwin, "Trump Touts His Loyalty to Wall Street, Coal Industry, and Guns," *New York Times*, April 28, 2017; Amy Davidson Sorkin, "Donald Trump's Worse Than You Think," *New Yorker*, January 9, 2016.

34 von Hoffman, *Citizen Cohn*, 354–360; In re Cohn, 118 A.D.2d 15 (N.Y. App. Div. 1986); Auletta, "Don't Mess with Roy Cohn," 48–52.

35 Matt Taibbi, "The Scorpion and the Frog: Donald Trump and Roy Cohn," *Rolling Stone*, May 20, 2016; Brenner, "How Donald Trump and Roy Cohn's Ruthless Symbiosis Changed America."

36 In re Cohn, 118 A.D.2d 15 (N.Y. App. Div. 1986); Zion, *The Autobiography of Roy Cohn*, 276–280.

37 Jeffrey Toobin, "Roger Stone, Political Provocateur," *New Yorker*, January 20, 2008; Roger Stone with Mike Colapietro, *The Man Who Killed Kennedy: The Case Against LBJ* (Skyhorse Publishing, 2013), 95.

38 Brenner, "How Donald Trump and Roy Cohn's Ruthless Symbiosis Changed America"; von Hoffman, *Citizen Cohn*, 432–436.

39 von Hoffman, *Citizen Cohn*, 432–438; Sam Roberts, "Roy Cohn, Aide to McCarthy and Fiery Lawyer, Dies at 59," *New York Times*, August 3, 1986.

40 Brenner, "How Donald Trump and Roy Cohn's Ruthless Symbiosis Changed America"; Mahler and Flegenheimer, "What Donald Trump Learned From Roy Cohn."

41 Michael S. Schmidt and Maggie Haberman, "'Where's My Roy Cohn?' Trump Asked as Mueller Closed In," *New York Times*, January 4, 2018; Bob Woodward, *Fear: Trump in the White House* (Simon & Schuster, 2018), 162–164.

42 Daniel Dale, "Trump Keeps Saying He's the President of Law and Order, but He Keeps Trying to Subvert the Law on Himself," *Washington Post*, July 12, 2020; Peter Baker, "Trump and the Politics of Dominance," *New York Times*, June 3, 2020.

43 Charlie Savage, "Barr Distorts Findings of Mueller Report," *New York Times*, April 19, 2019; Katie Benner, "Barr Undermined Justice Department's Independence," *New York Times*, January 14, 2021; Peter Baker, "Trump and Justice Dept. Lawyer Said to Have Plotted to Oust Acting Attorney General," *New York Times*, January 22, 2021.

44 Steven Levitsky and Daniel Ziblatt, *How Democracies Die* (Crown, 2018), 176–193; Michael Wolff, *Fire and Fury: Inside the Trump White House* (Henry Holt and Co., 2018), 304–312.

45 Taibbi, "The Scorpion and the Frog"; Brenner, "How Donald Trump and Roy Cohn's Ruthless Symbiosis Changed America"; Rich, "The Original Donald Trump."

CHAPTER 3

1 Jonah E. Bromwich and Ben Protess, "Top Trump Organization Executive Testifies against Firm He Helped Build," *New York Times*, November 15, 2022, https://www.nytimes.com/2022/11/15/nyregion/weisselberg-cfo-trump-organization.html.

2 U.S. Department of the Treasury, Bureau of the Fiscal Service, "Debt to the Penny," Fiscal Data through January 20, 2021, https://fiscaldata.treasury.gov/datasets/debt-to-the-penny/debt-to-the-penny.

3 David Barstow, Susanne Craig, and Russ Buettner, "Trump Engaged in Suspect Tax Schemes as He Reaped Riches from His Father," *New York Times*, October 2, 2018, https://www.nytimes.com/interactive/2018/10/02/us/politics/donald-trump-tax-schemes-fred-trump.html.

4 Ibid.

5 David Cay Johnston, *The Making of Donald Trump* (Melville House, 2016).

6 Clare O'Connor, "Fourth Time's a Charm: How Donald Trump Made Bankruptcy Work for Him," *Forbes*, April 29, 2011, https://www.forbes.com/sites/clareoconnor/2011/04/29/fourth-times-a-charm-how-donald-trump-made-bankruptcy-work-for-him/.

7 J. Michael Diehl, "I Sold Trump $100,000 Worth of Pianos. Then He Stiffed Me," *Washington Post*, September 28, 2016, https://www.washingtonpost.com/posteverything/wp/2016/09/28/i-sold-trump-100000-worth-of-pianos-then-he-stiffed-me/.

8 Steve Reilly, "Hundreds Allege Donald Trump Doesn't Pay His Bills," *USA Today*, June 9, 2016, https://www.usatoday.com/story/news/politics/elections/2016/06/09/donald-trump-unpaid-bills-republican-president-laswuits/85297274/.

9 Mark Wilson, "The Weirdest Products Donald Trump Has Ever Licensed," Fast Company, October 17, 2016, https://www.fastcompany.com/3064975/the-weirdest-products-donald-trump-has-ever-licensed.

10 Michael Isikoff, "'Trump University' Fraud Claims Surface in Campaign," Yahoo News, February 26, 2016, https://www.yahoo.com/news/trump-university-lawsuits-emerges-in-campaign-212931048.html

11 Camila Domonoske, "Judge Approves $25 Million Settlement of Trump University Lawsuit," NPR, March 31, 2017, https://www.npr.org/sections/thetwo-way/2017/03/31/522199535/judge-approves-25-million-settlement-of-trump-university-lawsuit.

12 Jane Mayer, "Donald Trump's Ghostwriter Tells All," *New Yorker*, July 25, 2016, https://www.newyorker.com/magazine/2016/07/25/donald-trumps-ghostwriter-tells-all.

13 Tony Schwartz, interview, *Good Morning America*, July 18, 2016, https://www.goodmorningamerica.com/news/story/tony-schwartz-author-donald-trumps-art-deal-trump-40662196.

14 "For 'Apprentice' Insiders, Trump's 2016 Bid Has Echoes of Reality TV," Reuters, March 23, 2016, https://www.reuters.com/article/world/for-apprentice-insiders-trump-s-2016-bid-has-echoes-of-reality-tv-idUSKCN0WP11C/.

15 David A. Fahrenthold, "Trump: A True Story," *Washington Post*, August 10, 2016, https://www.washingtonpost.com/graphics/politics/2016-election/trump-lies/.

16 Documentary footage cited in Marc Fisher and Michael Kranish, *Trump Revealed: An American Journey of Ambition, Ego, Money, and Power* (Scribner, 2017), 297.

17 Russ Buettner and Susanne Craig, "Decade in the Red: Trump Tax Figures Show over $1 Billion in Business Losses," *New York Times*, May 8, 2019, https://www.nytimes.com/interactive/2019/05/07/us/politics/donald-trump-taxes.html.

18 Michael Knigge, "Don't Retweet Trump and Don't Use His Language," interview

with George Lakoff, January 21, 2018, DW, https://www.dw.com/en/dont-retweet
-donald-trump-and-dont-use-his-language/a-42213110.

19 Isaac Chotiner, "Why Stuart Stevens Wants to Defeat Donald Trump," *New Yorker*, August 3, 2020, https://www.newyorker.com/news/q-and-a/why-stuart
-stevens-wants-to-defeat-donald-trump.

20 Peter Baker, "Once Critics of Trump, These Republicans Are Now Playing by His Rules," *New York Times*, May 23, 2024, https://www.nytimes.com/2024/05/23/us
/politics/trump-critics-endorsements.html.

CHAPTER 4

1 Sarah L. Kaufman, "Why Was Trump Lurking behind Clinton? How Body Language Dominated the Debate," *Washington Post*, October 10, 2016, https://www
.washingtonpost.com/news/arts-and-entertainment/wp/2016/10/10/why-was
-trump-lurking-behind-clinton-how-body-language-dominated-the-debate/.

2 Emily Schultheis, "Nebraska Senator Deb Fischer Re-Endorses Donald Trump after Tape Scandal," CBS News, October 12, 2016, https://www.cbsnews.com/news
/nebraska-senator-deb-fischer-re-endorses-donald-trump-after-tape-scandal/;
Aaron Blake, "Jason Chaffetz Just Set Some Sort of Modern Record for Flip-Floppery," *Washington Post*, October 26, 2016, https://www.washingtonpost.com/news
/the-fix/wp/2016/10/26/gop-rep-jason-chaffetz-says-his-conscience-wont-let
-him-support-donald-trump-just-vote-for-him/.

3 John A. Farrell, "Notes Indicate Nixon Interfered with 1968 Peace Talks," *Smithsonian Magazine*, January 2, 2017, https://www.smithsonianmag.com/smart-news
/notes-indicate-nixon-interfered-1968-peace-talks-180961627/.

4 Bill Moyers, "When the Republicans Really Were the Party of Lincoln," July 2, 2014, Bill Moyers.com, https://billmoyers.com/2014/07/02/when-the-republicans
-really-were-the-party-of-lincoln/.

5 Eugene Robinson, "Why Won't the GOP Compete for African American Votes?" History News Network, https://www.historynewsnetwork.org/article/eugene
-robinson-why-wont-the-gop-compete-for-afric.

6 Rick Perlstein, "Exclusive: Lee Atwater's Infamous 1981 Interview on the Southern Strategy," *The Nation*, November 13, 2012, https://www.thenation.com/article
/archive/exclusive-lee-atwaters-infamous-1981-interview-southern-strategy/.

7 LaKeshia N. Myers, "The Spirit of Lee Atwater Lingers among Us: How Critical Race Theory Became the GOP's New Southern Strategy," *Milwaukee Courier*, August 13, 2021, https://milwaukeecourieronline.com/index.php/2021/08/13/the
-spirit-of-lee-atwater-lingers-among-us-how-critical-race-theory-became-the
-gops-new-southern-strategy/.

8 Zinn Education Project, "Aug. 3, 1980: Reagan Gives 'State's Rights' Speech at Neshoba County Fair," August 4, 2023, https://www.zinnedproject.org/news/tdih
/reagan-speech-at-neshoba/.

9 Josh Levin, "Linda Taylor, Welfare Queen: Ronald Reagan Made Her a Notorious American Villain. Linda Taylor's Other Sins Were Far Worse," *Slate*, December 19, 2013, https://www.slate.com/articles/news_and_politics/history/2013/12/linda
_taylor_welfare_queen_ronald_reagan_made_her_a_notorious_american_vil
lain.html.

10 John Blake, "Return of the 'Welfare Queen,'" *CNN Politics*, January 23, 2012, https://
www.cnn.com/2012/01/23/politics/weflare-queen/index.html.

11 Thom Hartmann, "Trump to the GOP Is Like a Parasitic Wasp Is to a Caterpillar,"

Raw Story, August 24, 2023, https://www.rawstory.com/raw-investigates/trump-parasite/. This analysis examines the parasitic relationship between Trump and the traditional Republican establishment.

12 "Language: A Key Mechanism of Control," FAIR.org, September 5, 2018, https://fair.org/home/language-a-key-mechanism-of-control/.

13 Andrew Prokop, "How Fox News Evolved into a Propaganda Operation," Vox, March 22, 2019, https://www.vox.com/2019/3/22/18275835/fox-news-trump-propaganda-tom-rosenstiel.

14 Fairleigh Dickinson University, "Some News Leaves People Knowing Less," Public-Mind Poll, November 21, 2011, https://publicmind.fdu.edu/2011/knowless/.

15 McKay Coppins, "'Combative, Tribal, Angry': Newt Gingrich Set the Stage for Trump," NPR, November 1, 2018, https://www.npr.org/2018/11/01/662906525/combative-tribal-angry-newt-gingrich-set-the-stage-for-trump-journalist-says.

16 Thomas E. Mann and Norman J. Ornstein, "Let's Just Say It: The Republicans Are the Problem," Washington Post, April 27, 2012, https://www.washingtonpost.com/opinions/lets-just-say-it-the-republicans-are-the-problem/2012/04/27/gIQAxCVUlT_story.html.

17 Robert Draper, Do Not Ask What Good We Do: Inside the U.S. House of Representatives (Free Press, 2012), 18–19. This book, based on extensive interviews with those present, documents the inauguration night meeting and subsequent Republican strategy.

18 Frank James, "Sen. Mitch McConnell Insists: One and Done for Obama," NPR, November 4, 2010, https://www.npr.org/sections/itsallpolitics/2010/11/04/131069048/sen-mcconnell-insists-one-term-for-obama.

19 Jane Mayer, "Covert Operations: The Billionaire Brothers Who Are Waging a War against Obama," New Yorker, August 30, 2010, https://www.newyorker.com/magazine/2010/08/30/covert-operations.

20 Suzanne Goldenberg, "Tea Party Movement: Billionaire Koch Brothers Who Helped It Grow," The Guardian, October 13, 2010, https://www.theguardian.com/world/2010/oct/13/tea-party-billionaire-koch-brothers.

21 Christopher Parker, "The Tea Party, Still Brewing," UW College of Arts & Sciences, October 2012, https://artsci.washington.edu/news/2012-10/tea-party-still-brewing.

22 Krissah Thompson, "NAACP Backs Report That Ties Racist Groups to Tea Party," Washington Post, October 20, 2010, http://www.washingtonpost.com/wp-dyn/content/article/2010/10/20/AR2010102004020.html.

23 Jason M. Breslow, "Bob Inglis: Climate Change and the Republican Party," PBS Frontline, October 24, 2012, https://www.pbs.org/wgbh/frontline/article/bob-inglis-climate-change-and-the-republican-party/.

24 David Daley, "The Redistricting Landscape, 2021–22," Brennan Center for Justice, February 11, 2021, https://www.brennancenter.org/our-work/research-reports/redistricting-landscape-2021–22.

25 Jonathan Martin, "Grover Norquist, the Anti-Tax Enforcer, Faces Big Test," New York Times, November 19, 2012, https://www.nytimes.com/2012/11/20/us/politics/grover-norquist-author-of-antitax-pledge-faces-big-test.html.

26 "The Lugar Center and McCourt School Unveil Bipartisan Index Rankings for the 117th Congress," McCourt School of Public Policy, Georgetown University, May 3, 2022, https://mccourt.georgetown.edu/news/bipartisan-index-rankings-117th-congress/.

27 Congressional Research Service, "The Economic Effects of the 2017 Tax Revision:

Preliminary Observations," May 22, 2019, https://sgp.fas.org/crs/misc/R45736.pdf.

28 Rebecca R. Ruiz, Robert Gebeloff, Steve Eder, and Ben Protess, "A Conservative Agenda Unleashed on the Federal Courts," New York Times, March 14, 2020, https://www.nytimes.com/2020/03/14/us/trump-appeals-court-judges.html.

29 "An Examination of the 2016 Electorate, Based on Validated Voters," Pew Research Center, August 9, 2018, https://www.pewresearch.org/politics/2018/08/09/an-examination-of-the-2016-electorate-based-on-validated-voters/. This comprehensive study confirms that "Trump won by more than two-to-one (64 percent to 28 percent)" among white voters without a college degree, who made up 44 percent of the electorate.

30 "Lindsey Graham: Donald Trump Is a 'Race-Baiting, Xenophobic Religious Bigot,'" CNN video, December 8, 2015, https://www.cnn.com/videos/politics/2015/12/08/lindsey-graham-donald-trump-xenophobic-bigot-interview-newday.cnn.

31 Robert Kagan, "Our Constitutional Crisis Is Already Here," Washington Post, September 23, 2021, https://www.washingtonpost.com/opinions/2021/09/23/robert-kagan-constitutional-crisis/.

CHAPTER 5

1 Kayla Kitson, "The Koch Brothers' Best Investment," The American Prospect, June 28, 2018, https://prospect.org/power/koch-brothers-best-investment/.

2 "Koch Brothers Could Get Up to $1.4 Billion Tax Cut from Law They Helped Pass," Americans for Tax Fairness, January 10, 2024, https://americansfortaxfairness.org/koch-brothers-1-billion-tax-cut/.

3 Citizens United v. Federal Election Commission, 558 U.S. 310 (2010), Federal Election Commission, "Citizens United v. FEC," https://www.fec.gov/legal-resources/court-cases/citizens-united-v-fec/.

4 Karl Evers-Hillstrom, "More Money, Less Transparency: A Decade under Citizens United," OpenSecrets, January 14, 2020, https://www.opensecrets.org/news/reports/a-decade-under-citizens-united.

5 Ibid.

6 Gregory Zuckerman and Richard Rubin, "James Simons, Robert Mercer, Others at Renaissance to Pay up to $7 Billion to Settle Tax Probe," Wall Street, Journal, September 2, 2021, https://www.wsj.com/finance/investing/james-simons-robert-mercer-others-at-renaissance-to-pay-7-billion-to-settle-tax-probe-11630617328.

7 Peter Stone, "Sheldon Adelson to Donate $100m to Trump and Republicans, Fundraisers Say," The Guardian, February 10, 2020, https://www.theguardian.com/us-news/2020/feb/10/sheldon-adelson-trump-donation-republicans-congress.

8 Bill Chappell, "Former Trump Campaign Head Manafort Was Paid Millions by a Putin Ally, AP Says," NPR, March 22, 2017, https://www.npr.org/sections/thetwo-way/2017/03/22/521088772/former-trump-campaign-head-manafort-was-paid-millions-by-a-putin-ally-ap-says.

9 Jane Mayer, "The Reclusive Hedge-Fund Tycoon Behind the Trump Presidency," New Yorker, March 17, 2017, https://www.newyorker.com/magazine/2017/03/27/the-reclusive-hedge-fund-tycoon-behind-the-trump-presidency.

10 "Newly Published Cambridge Analytica Documents Show Unlawful Support for Trump in 2016," Campaign Legal Center, accessed May 2025, https://campaignlegal.org/update/newly-published-cambridge-analytica-documents-show-unlawful-support-trump-2016; Carole Cadwalladr and Emma Graham-Harrison, "Revealed: 50 Million Facebook Profiles Harvested for Cambridge Analytica in

Major Data Breach," March 17, 2018, *The Guardian*, https://www.theguardian.com /news/2018/mar/17/cambridge-analytica-facebook-influence-us-election.

11 "Robert Mercer," Center for Media and Democracy, *Sourcewatch*, accessed May 9, 2025, https://www.sourcewatch.org/index.php/Robert_Mercer.

12 Donald J. Trump, "Remarks by President Trump at Signing of H.R. 1, Tax Cuts and Jobs Bill Act," White House Archives, December 22, 2017, https://trump whitehouse.archives.gov/briefings-statements/remarks-president-trump -signing-h-r-1-tax-cuts-jobs-bill-act-h-r-1370/.

13 Damian J. Troise, "US Companies' Tax Windfall Fuels Record Share Buybacks," AP News, April 28, 2021, https://apnews.com/article/438fae12f9204b1fbd8e8b1985 ae554f.

14 Jane G. Gravelle and Donald J. Marples, "The Economic Effects of the 2017 Tax Revision: Preliminary Observations," Congressional Research Service, June 7, 2019, https://crsreports.congress.gov/product/pdf/R/R45736.

15 Allan Holmes, Peter Cary, Joe Yerardi, and Chris Zubak-Skees, "Did Billionaires Pay Off Republicans for Passing the Trump Tax Bill?" Center for Public Integrity, February 28, 2023, https://publicintegrity.org/inequality-poverty-opportunity/taxes /trumps-tax-cuts/did-billionaires-pay-off-republicans-for-passing-the-trump -tax-bill/.

16 Jon Queally, "After Spending $20 Million to Pass #GOPTaxScam, Koch Bros to Save More Than $1 Billion This Year," Common Dreams, January 24, 2018, https://www.commondreams.org/news/2018/01/24/after-spending-20-million -pass-goptaxscam-koch-bros-save-more-1-billion-year.

17 Molly Coleman, "The Next Trump Judges Will Be So Much Worse," Balls and Strikes, January 22, 2025, https://ballsandstrikes.org/nominations/next-trump -judges-so-much-worse/.

18 Juliet Eilperin, Brady Dennis, and John Muyskens, "Trump Rolled Back More Than 125 Environmental Safeguards. Here's How," *Washington Post*, October 30, 2020, https://www.washingtonpost.com/graphics/2020/climate-environment/trump -climate-environment-protections/.

19 Elizabeth Schulze, Will Steakin, and Allison Pecorin, "As Musk, Trump Administration target CFPB, Democrats Defend Consumer Watchdog's Impact," ABC News, February 10, 2025, https://abcnews.go.com/Politics/musk-trump-admin istration-target-cfpb-democrats-tout-consumer/story?id=118664275.

20 Jake Johnson, "In 'Latest Attempt to Distort Democracy,' Koch Brothers Bolster GOP Tax Cut Efforts," Common Dreams, July 31, 2017, https://www.common dreams.org/news/2017/07/31/latest-attempt-distort-democracy-koch-brothers -bolster-gop-tax-cut-efforts.

21 David Armiak and Alex Kotch, "Republican AGs Cannot Shake Ties to Violent Trump Coup Attempt," Truthout, January 15, 2021, https://truthout.org/articles /republican-ags-cannot-shake-ties-to-violent-trump-coup-attempt/.

22 Pema Levy, "New Report Reveals the Shadowy Money Behind the Plot to Overturn the Election," *Mother Jones*, October 24, 2024, https://www.motherjones.com/poli tics/2024/10/non-citizen-voting/.

23 James Oliphant, Jason Lange, Julia Harte, and Tim Reid, "Republican Donations Surge Despite Corporate Boycott after Capitol Riots," Reuters, March 9, 2021, https://www.reuters.com/article/world/republican-donations-surge-despite -corporate-boycott-after-capitol-riots-idUSKBN2B119A/.

24 This quote comes from a July 28, 2015, interview on my radio program. The audio is available at https://www.youtube.com/watch?v=hDsPWmioSHg.

CHAPTER 6

1 Nick Miroff and Robert Moore, "7-year-old Migrant Girl Taken into Border Patrol Custody Dies of Dehydration, Exhaustion," *Washington Post*, December 13, 2018, https://www.washingtonpost.com/world/national-security/7-year-old-mi grant-girl-taken-into-border-patrol-custody-dies-of-dehydration-exhaustion /2018/12/13/8909e356-ff03-11e8-862a-b6a6f3ce8199_story.html.

2 Ibid.

3 Steven T. Dennis, "Private Prison Stocks Soar after Trump Win," *Bloomberg*, November 7, 2024, https://www.bloomberg.com/news/articles/2024-11-07/private -prison-stocks-soar-after-trump-win-on-deportation-plans.

4 Josh Dawsey, "Trump Derides Protections for Immigrants from 'Shithole' Countries," *Washington Post*, January 12, 2018, https://www.washingtonpost.com/pol itics/trump-attacks-protections-for-immigrants-from-shithole-countries-in-oval -office-meeting/2018/01/11/bfc0725c-f711-11e7-91af-31ac729add94_story.html.

5 Julia Ainsley, Jacob Soboroff, and Geoff Bennett, "Trump Admin Separated Thousands More Migrant Children Than Originally Reported," NBC News, January 17, 2019, https://www.nbcnews.com/news/us-news/thousands-more-migrant-children -were-separated-parents-under-trump-n958811.

6 Madison Pauly, "Trump's Immigration Crackdown Is a Boom Time for Private Prisons," *Mother Jones*, May/June 2018, https://www.motherjones.com/poli tics/2018/05/trumps-immigration-crackdown-is-a-boom-time-for-private-pri sons/.

7 Priscilla Alvarez, "John Kelly Joins Board of Company Operating Largest Shelter for Unaccompanied Migrant Children," CBS News, May 3, 2019, https://www.cbsnews .com/news/john-kelly-joins-board-of-caliburn-international-company-operating -largest-unaccompanied-migrant-children-shelter/.

8 Amanda Hernández, "For-Profit Immigration Detention Expands as Trump Accelerates His Deportation Plans," Stateline, April 11, 2025, https://stateline.org /2025/04/11/for-profit-immigration-detention-expands-as-trump-accelerates-his -deportation-plans/.

9 Bethany Carson and Eleana Diaz, "Payoff: How Congress Ensures Private Prison Profit with an Immigrant Detention Quota," Grassroots Leadership, April 2015, https://inthepublicinterest.org/wp-content/uploads/Payoff-How-Congress -Ensures-Private-Prison-Profit.pdf.

10 Nicole Acevedo, "Why Are Migrant Children Dying in U.S. Custody?," NBC News, May 29, 2019, https://www.nbcnews.com/news/latino/why-are-migrant -children-dying-u-s-custody-n1010316.

11 Nadja Popovich, Livia Albeck-Ripka, and Kendra Pierre-Louis, "The Trump Administration Rolled Back More Than 100 Environmental Rules. Here's the Full List," *New York Times*, January 20, 2021, https://www.nytimes.com/interactive/2020 /climate/trump-environment-rollbacks-list.html.

12 Jeff Stein and Elizabeth Dwoskin, "Trump Taps Musk, Ramaswamy to Lead 'Department of Government Efficiency,'" *Washington Post*, November 12, 2024, https://www.washingtonpost.com/business/2024/11/12/elon-musk-trump-doge -vivek-ramaswamy/.

13 Marie Brenner, "How Donald Trump and Roy Cohn's Ruthless Symbiosis Changed America," *Vanity Fair*, June 28, 2017, https://www.vanityfair.com/news/2017/06/donald-trump-roy-cohn-relationship.

14 Charlie Savage, "Trump Declares a National Emergency, and Provokes a Constitutional Clash," *New York Times*, February 15, 2019, https://www.nytimes.com/2019/02/15/us/politics/national-emergency-trump.html.

15 Adam Serwer, "The Cruelty Is the Point," *The Atlantic*, October 3, 2018, https://www.theatlantic.com/ideas/archive/2018/10/the-cruelty-is-the-point/572104/.

16 Steffie Woolhandler, David U. Himmelstein, Sameer Ahmed, Zinzi Bailey, Mary T. Bassett, Michael Bird et al., "Public Policy and Health in the Trump Era," *The Lancet*, February 20, 2021, https://www.thelancet.com/journals/lancet/article/PIIS0140-6736(20)32545-9/abstract.

17 Robert Costa and Philip Rucker, "Woodward Book: Trump Says He Knew Coronavirus Was 'Deadly' and Worse Than the Flu While Intentionally Misleading Americans," *Washington Post*, September 9, 2020, https://www.washingtonpost.com/politics/bob-woodward-rage-book-trump/2020/09/09/0368fe3c-efd2-11ea-b4bc-3a2098fc73d4_story.html.

18 Chuck Collins, "U.S. Billionaire Wealth Surpasses $1.1 Trillion Gain Since Mid-March," Institute for Policy Studies, December 9, 2020, https://ips-dc.org/10-months-in-us-billionaire-wealth-surpasses-1-1trillion/.

19 Sydney Lupkin, "How Operation Warp Speed's Big Vaccine Contracts Could Stay Secret," NPR, September 29, 2020, https://www.npr.org/sections/health-shots/2020/09/29/917899357/how-operation-warp-speeds-big-vaccine-contracts-could-stay-secret.

20 Jonathan O'Connell, Aaron Gregg, and Steven Rich, "Treasury, SBA Data Show Small-Business Loans Went to Private-Equity Backed Chains, Members of Congress," *Washington Post*, July 6, 2020, https://www.washingtonpost.com/business/2020/07/06/sba-ppp-loans-data/.

21 Kathryn Watson, "Trump Removes Inspector General Who Was to Oversee $2 Trillion Stimulus Spending," CBS News, April 7, 2020, https://www.cbsnews.com/news/trump-removes-inspector-general-glenn-fine-stimulus-spending/.

22 Sylvan Lane, "Four Senators Sold Stocks before Coronavirus Threat Crashed Market," *The Hill*, March 20, 2020, https://thehill.com/homenews/senate/488593-four-senators-sold-stocks-before-coronavirus-threat-crashed-market/.

23 Popovich, Albeck-Ripka, and Pierre-Louis, "The Trump Administration Rolled Back More Than 100 Environmental Rules."

24 Lisa Friedman, "A Coal Executive's 'Action Plan' for Trump Is Made Public," *New York Times*, January 9, 2018, https://www.nytimes.com/2018/01/09/climate/coal-murray-trump-memo.html.

25 Popovich, Albeck-Ripka, and Pierre-Louis, "The Trump Administration Rolled Back More Than 100 Environmental Rules."

26 The Indigenous Environmental Network, "The Indigenous Environmental Network Responds to Executive Orders for Approving KXL & DAPL," January 24, 2017, www.ienearth.org/the-indigenous-environmental-network-responds-to-executive-orders-for-approving-kxl-dapl/.

27 Aaron Gregg, "Defense Spending Has Increased Nearly 20 Percent in the Trump Years," *Washington Post*, October 13, 2020, https://www.washingtonpost.com/business/2020/10/13/defense-contractors-stock-performance/.

28 Karoun Demirjian and Colby Itkowitz, "Trump Vetoes Congress's Attempt to

Block Arms Sales to Saudi Arabia," *Washington Post*, July 24, 2019, https://www
.washingtonpost.com/politics/trump-vetoes-congresss-attempt-to-block-arms
-sales-to-saudi-arabia/2019/07/24/7b047c32-ae65-11e9-a0c9-6d2d7818f3da_story
.html.

29 Nick Miroff and Josh Dawsey, "North Dakota Company That Trump Touted Gets
$400 Million Border Wall Contract," *Washington Post*, December 2, 2019, https://
www.washingtonpost.com/immigration/north-dakota-company-that-trump
-touted-gets-400-million-border-wall-contract/2019/12/02/9c661132-1568-11ea
-bf81-ebe89f477d1e_story.html.

30 Tristan Greene, "Study: Trump's Paid Peter Thiel's Palantir $1.5B So Far to Build
ICE's Mass Surveillance Network," The Next Web, August 8, 2019, https://thenext
web.com/news/study-trumps-paid-peter-thiels-palantir-1-5b-so-far-to-build-ices
-mass-surveillance-network.

31 Jonathan Levinson and Conrad Wilson, "Federal Officers Use Unmarked Vehicles to Grab People in Portland, DHS Confirms," NPR, July 17, 2020, https://
www.npr.org/2020/07/17/892277592/federal-officers-use-unmarked-vehicles
-to-grab-protesters-in-portland.

32 Stephen Gandel, "Maker of Tear Gas Used on D.C. Protesters Gets Millions from
Federal Government," CBS News, June 8, 2020, https://www.cbsnews.com/news
/tear-gas-maker-washington-d-c-protesters-millions-federal-government/.

33 Citizens for Responsibility and Ethics in Washington, "This Sedition Is Brought
to You By. . .," January 3, 2022, https://www.citizensforethics.org/reports-investiga
tions/crew-reports/this-sedition-is-brought-to-you-by/.

34 Angela Li and Caitlin Moniz, " Corporations Have Given over $50 million to
the Sedition Caucus," CREW, January 6, 2023, https://www.citizensforethics.org
/reports-investigations/crew-reports/corporations-have-given-over-50-million
-to-the-sedition-caucus/.

CHAPTER 7

1 U.S. House of Representatives, Select Committee to Investigate the January 6th
Attack on the United States Capitol, Public Hearing on the January 6th Attack,
117th Cong., 2nd sess., June 21, 2022, testimony of Ruby Freeman. Video available
at: https://www.c-span.org/video/?521387-1/house-committee-hearing-january
-6-capitol-attack. Also reported by NPR: Deepa Shivaram, "Shaye Moss Staffed
an Election Office in Georgia. Then She Was Targeted by Trump," NPR, June 22,
2022, https://www.npr.org/2022/06/22/1106459556/shaye-moss-staffed-an-election
-office-in-georgia-then-she-was-targeted-by-trump.

2 Georgia Secretary of State's Office, statements by Gabriel Sterling (Voting System
Implementation Manager) and Frances Watson (Chief Investigator), December 2020. Documentation available at: "Jan. 6th Committee Releases Full Testimony of Fulton County Election Workers," Fox5 Atlanta, December 29, 2022,
https://www.fox5atlanta.com/news/jan-6th-committee-releases-full-testimony
-of-fulton-county-election-workers.

3 "Fact Check: Video from Georgia Does NOT Show Suitcases Filled with Ballots
Suspiciously Pulled from Under a Table; Poll Watchers Were NOT Told to Leave,"
Lead Stories, December 4, 2020, https://leadstories.com/hoax-alert/2020/12/fact
-check-video-from-ga-does-not-show-suitcases-filled-with-ballots-pulled-from
-under-a-table-after-poll-workers-dismissed.html.

4 Amy Gardner, "'I Just Want to Find 11,780 Votes': In Extraordinary Hour-Long
Call, Trump Pressures Georgia Secretary of State to Recalculate the Vote in His

Favor," *Washington Post*, January 3, 2021, https://www.washingtonpost.com/pol itics/trump-raffensperger-call-georgia-vote/2021/01/03/d45acb92-4dc4-11eb -bda4-615aaefd0555_story.html. Full audio available at: https://www.washington post.com/politics/trump-raffensperger-call-transcript-georgia-vote/2021/01/03 /2768e0cc-4ddd-11eb-83e3-322644d82356_story.html.

5   Testimony of Wandrea "Shaye" Moss, House Select Committee to Investigate the January 6th Attack on the United States Capitol, Hearing, June 21, 2022. Video available at: https://www.c-span.org/video/?521387-1/house-committee-hearing -january-6-capitol-attack. Also reported by NPR: Jaclyn Diaz, "Rudy Giuliani Concedes He Made False Statements Against 2 Georgia Election Workers," NPR, July 26, 2023, https://www.npr.org/2023/07/26/1190173929/rudy-giuliani-georgia -election-workers and NBC News: Ryan J. Reilly, Summer Concepcion, Dareh Gregorian, and Victoria Ebner, "Jury to Decide How Much Rudy Giuliani Must Pay Election Workers He Defamed," NBC News, December 11, 2023, https://www .nbcnews.com/politics/politics-news/jury-decide-much-rudy-giuliani-must-pay -election-workers-defamed-rcna128940.

6   Testimony of Ruby Freeman, House Select Committee to Investigate the January 6th Attack on the United States Capitol, Hearing, June 21, 2022. Video available at: https://www.c-span.org/video/?521387-1/house-committee-hearing-january -6-capitol-attack. Also reported by *The Washington Post*: Amy Gardner, "Elec- tion Workers Describe 'Hateful' Threats after Trump's False Claims," June 21, 2022, https://www.washingtonpost.com/national-security/2022/06/21/ruby-freeman -shaye-moss-jan6-testimony/.

7   Ibid. Freeman's emotional testimony also reported by *BuzzFeed News*: Stephanie K. Baer, "A Georgia Elections Worker and Her Mom Described How Trump's Lies about Voter Fraud Tore Their Lives Apart," *BuzzFeed News*, June 21, 2022, https://www.buzzfeednews.com/article/skbaer/georgia-elections-worker-mom -jan-6-testimony; National Public Radio: https://www.npr.org/2022/06/21/110584 8096/jan-6-committee-hearing-transcript.

8   Glenn Kessler, Salvador Rizzo, and Meg Kelly, "Trump's False or Misleading Claims Total 30,573 over 4 years," *Washington Post*, January 24, 2021, https:// www.washingtonpost.com/politics/2021/01/24/trumps-false-or-misleading -claims-total-30573-over-four-years/.

9   Carlos Lozada, "20 Ways to Recognize Tyranny—and Fight It," *Washington Post*, February 24, 2017, https://www.washingtonpost.com/news/book-party/wp/2017 /02/24/20-ways-to-recognize-tyranny-and-fight-it/.

10 Aaron Blake, "Kellyanne Conway Says Donald Trump's Team Has 'Alternative Facts.' Which Pretty Much Says It All," *Washington Post*, January 22, 2017, https:// www.washingtonpost.com/news/the-fix/wp/2017/01/22/kellyanne-conway-says -donald-trumps-team-has-alternate-facts-which-pretty-much-says-it-all/.

11 Michael Barbaro, "Donald Trump Clung to 'Birther' Lie for Years, and Still Isn't Apologetic," *New York Times*, September 16, 2016, https://www.nytimes.com/2016 /09/17/us/politics/donald-trump-obama-birther.html.

12 Susan Crabtree, "Obama on Birther Issue: 'We Don't Have Time for This Silli- ness,'" Talking Points Memo, April 27, 2011, https://talkingpointsmemo.com/dc /obama-on-birther-issue-we-don-t-have-time-for-this-silliness.

13 Ashley Parker and Steve Eder, "Inside the Six Weeks Donald Trump Was a Non- stop 'Birther,'" *New York Times*, July 2, 2016, https://www.nytimes.com/2016/07/03 /us/politics/donald-trump-birther-obama.html.

14 Masha Gessen, "The Putin Paradigm," *New York Review of Books*, December 13, 2016, https://www.nybooks.com/daily/2016/12/13/putin-paradigm-how-trump-will-rule/.

15 Steve Schmidt, interview by Brian Williams, *The 11th Hour*, MSNBC, January 30, 2018, clip available at: https://www.msnbc.com/msnbc/watch/schmidt-trump-2018 -state-of-the-union-speech-given-from-alternate-reality-1149997123694.

16 Hannah Arendt, *The Origins of Totalitarianism* (Harcourt, 1951), 474. This widely cited quote about totalitarianism can be verified at https://www.goodreads.com /work/quotes/23497-the-origins-of-totalitarianism, where Arendt identifies the ideal subject of totalitarian rule as someone for whom the distinction between fact and fiction no longer exists.

17 Donald Trump, "Remarks at the White House," November 4, 2020. Transcript available at: https://www.rev.com/blog/transcripts/donald-trump-2020-election -night-speech-transcript.

18 William Cummings, Joey Garrison, and Jim Sergent, "By the Numbers: President Donald Trump's Failed Efforts to Overturn the Election," *USA Today*, January 6, 2021, https://www.usatoday.com/in-depth/news/politics/elections/2021/01/06 /trumps-failed-efforts-overturn-election-numbers/4130307001/.

19 "Transcript and Audio: Trump Call With Georgia Election Officials," *Washington Post*, January 5, 2021, https://www.washingtonpost.com/politics/trump-raffen sperger-call-transcript-georgia-vote/2021/01/03/2768e0cc-4ddd-11eb-83e3-32 2644d82356_story.html.

20 Marshall Cohen, Zachary Cohen, and Dan Merica, "Trump Campaign Officials, Led by Rudy Giuliani, Oversaw Fake Electors Plot in 7 States," *CNN Politics*, January 20, 2022, https://www.cnn.com/2022/01/20/politics/trump-campaign-officials -rudy-giuliani-fake-electors/index.html.

21 Cybersecurity & Infrastructure Security Agency, "Joint Statement from Elections Infrastructure Government Coordinating Council & the Election Infrastructure Sector Coordinating Executive Committees," November 12, 2020, https:// www.cisa.gov/news-events/news/joint-statement-elections-infrastructure -government-coordinating-council-election. Statement archived at: https://web .archive.org/web/20201112184633/https://www.cisa.gov/news/2020/11/12 /joint-statement-elections-infrastructure-government-coordinating-council -election

22 Patrick Healy and Jeremy W. Peters, "Donald Trump Won't Say If He'll Accept Result of Election," *New York Times*, October 19, 2016, https://www.nytimes.com /2016/10/20/us/politics/presidential-debate.html. Video available at: https://www .youtube.com/watch?v=cP0G4vJ5OMw.

23 Jay O'Brien, Arthur Jones II, and Doc Louallen, "Former Capitol Police Officer Wants to End the Falsehoods about Jan. 6," ABC News, October 5, 2024, https:// abcnews.go.com/Politics/former-capitol-police-officer-end-falsehoods-jan-6 /story?id=114464816.

24 Ryan J. Reilly, "For Jan. 6 Rioters Who Believed Trump, Storming the Capitol Made Sense," NBC News, June 20, 2022, https://www.nbcnews.com/news/amp/rc na33125.

25 Donald J. Trump, Video Statement, January 6, 2021. Transcript available at https:// www.rev.com/transcripts/trump-video-telling-protesters-at-capitol-building-to -go-home-transcript.

26 Karen Yourish, Larry Buchanan, and Denise Lu, "The 147 Republicans Who Voted to Overturn Election Results," *New York Times*, January 7, 2021, https://www .nytimes.com/interactive/2021/01/07/us/elections/electoral-college-biden-objec tors.html.

27 Al Schmidt, Testimony, U.S. Senate Committee on Rules and Administration,

October 26, 2021, https://www.rules.senate.gov/hearings/emerging-threats-to-election-administration.

28 Katie Shepherd, "Armed Protesters Alleging Voter Fraud Surrounded the Home of Michigan's Secretary of State," *Washington Post*, December 7, 2020, https://www.washingtonpost.com/nation/2020/12/07/michigan-sos-benson-armed-protest/.

29 Gabriel Sterling, Press Conference, YouTube, December 1, 2020, https://www.youtube.com/watch?v=jLi-Yo6IucQ.

30 Jan Wolfe, "Four Officers Who Responded to U.S. Capitol Attack Have Died by Suicide," Reuters, August 2, 2021, https://www.reuters.com/world/us/officer-who-responded-us-capitol-attack-is-third-die-by-suicide-2021-08-02/.

31 Andrew Kaczynski and Melanie Zanona, "In Days after January 6, McCarthy said Trump Admitted Bearing Some Responsibility for Capitol Attack," CNN, January 14, 2022, https://www.cnn.com/2022/01/14/politics/kfile-kevin-mccarthy-donald-trump-january-6/index.html.

32 Kelsey Snell and Barbara Spruntat, "'The Mob Was Fed Lies': McConnell Rebukes Trump For His Role in Capitol Riot," NPR, January 19, 2021, https://www.npr.org/sections/trump-impeachment-effort-live-updates/2021/01/19/958410118/mcconnell-trump-provoked-mob-that-attacked-capitol.

33 "Voting Laws Roundup: December 2021," Brennan Center for Justice, January 12, 2022, https://www.brennancenter.org/our-work/research-reports/voting-laws-roundup-december-2021.

34 Olivia Rubin, "What Fox News Hosts Allegedly Said Privately versus On-Air about False Election Fraud Claims," ABC News, April 24, 2023, https://abcnews.go.com/Politics/fox-news-hosts-allegedly-privately-versus-air-false/story?id=97662551.

Chapter 8

1 "Voter Purges," Brennan Center for Justice, https://www.brennancenter.org/issues/ensure-every-american-can-vote/vote-suppression/voter-purges.

2 "The 2024 Anti-Democracy Playbook," American Oversight, https://americanoversight.org/resource/the-2024-anti-democracy-playbook/.

3 Greg Palast, "Trump Lost. Vote Suppression Won," San Diego Voice & Viewpoint, January 31, 2025, https://sdvoice.info/trump-lost-vote-suppression-won-here-are-the-numbers/.

4 Ashley Lopez, "Despite Mail Voting Changes, Ballot Rejections Remain Relatively Low in 2022 Midterms," NPR, January 13, 2023, https://www.npr.org/2023/01/13/1148799521/mail-ballot-rejection-rates-state-tally.

5 Palast, "Trump Lost."

6 "Election Administration and Voting Survey (EAVS) Comprehensive Report," U.S. Election Assistance Commission, May 28, 2025, https://www.eac.gov/research-and-data/studies-and-reports.

7 Palast, "Trump Lost."

8 Pat McCarthy, Steve Hobbs, and Lori Augino, "Ballot Tracking Can Improve Rejection-Rate Disparities," *Seattle Times*, May 16, 2022, https://www.seattletimes.com/opinion/ballot-tracking-can-improve-rejection-rate-disparities/.

9 Jane C. Timm, Rezwana Uddin, and Andrew Arenge, "In Key Battlegrounds, Voters of Color See Ballots Marked for Rejection at Higher Rates," NBC News, November 4, 2020, https://www.nbcnews.com/politics/2020-election/key-battlegrounds-voters-color-see-ballots-marked-rejection-higher-rates-n1245583.

10 "Purging Voter Rolls," Everything Policy, https://www.everythingpolicy.org/pol
    icy-briefs/purging-voter-rolls.

11 Greg Palast, "Court Approves Vigilante Mass Voter Challenges—Devastating
    Threat to 2024 Election," Greg Palast.com, October 24, 2024, https://www.greg
    palast.com/court-approves-vigilante-mass-voter-challengesdevastating-threat-to
    -2024-election/.

12 Mark Gruenburg, "Progressives to Air Vigilantes, Inc., Exposing Right-Wing
    Challenge to 851,000 Voters," *People's World*, October 7, 2024, https://peoplesworld
    .org/article/progressives-to-air-vigilantes-inc-exposing-rightwing-challenge-to
    -851000-voters/.

13 Palast, "Court Approves Vigilante Mass Voter Challenges."

14 Marc Elias, "The Growing Threat of Republican Election Vigilantes," Democracy
    Docket, September 14, 2023, https://www.democracydocket.com/opinion/the
    -growing-threat-of-republican-election-vigilantes/.

15 Sophie Chou, ProPublica, and Tyler Dukes, "In North Carolina, Black Voters'
    Mail-In Ballots Much More Likely to Be Rejected Than Those from Any Other
    Race," ProPublica, October 16, 2020, https://www.propublica.org/article/in-north
    -carolina-black-voters-mail-in-ballots-much-more-likely-to-be-rejected-than
    -those-from-any-other-race.

16 Natalia Contreras, "Voters of Color Had Mail-In Ballots Rejected at Higher Rates
    Than White Voters in Texas' March Primary," *Texas Tribune*, October 20, 2022,
    https://www.texastribune.org/2022/10/20/voting-texas-ballot-rejections/.

17 "Election Administration and Voting Survey (EAVS) Comprehensive Report,"
    U.S. Election Assistance Commission, https://www.eac.gov/research-and-data
    /studies-and-reports.

18 Palast, "Trump Lost."

19 Ibid.

20 Ibid.

21 "Voter Purges."

22 Greg Palast, "Vigilantes Inc: The Shocking Truth about the 2024 Election," Febru-
    ary 7, 2025, https://www.gregpalast.com/vigilantes-inc-the-shocking-truth-about
    -the-2024-election/.

CHAPTER 9

1 Annie Nova, Lorie Konish, Greg Iacurci, and Ana Teresa Solá, "Trump, DOGE
   Mass Job Cuts: Federal Workers' Money Questions Answered," CNBC, February
   21, 2025, https://www.cnbc.com/2025/02/21/trump-doge-mass-job-cuts-federal
   -workers-money-questions-answered.html.

2 Natasha Korecki, " 'You Lose All Hope': Federal Workers Gripped by Mental
   Health Distress Amid Trump Cuts," NBC News, March 10, 2025, https://www
   .nbcnews.com/politics/doge/federal-workers-gripped-mental-health-instability
   -trump-cutsrcna194485.

3 Philip Rucker and Robert Costa, "Bannon: Trump Administration Is in Unending
   Battle for 'Deconstruction of the Administrative State,'" *Washington Post*, February 23, 2017, https://www.washingtonpost.com/news/powerpost/wp/2017/02/23
   /bannon-trump-administration-is-in-unending-battle-for-deconstruction-of-the
   -administrative-state/.

4 The White House, "Establishing And Implementing the President's 'Department

of Government Efficiency,'" Executive Order 14158, January 20, 2025, https://www
.whitehouse.gov/presidential-actions/2025/01/establishing-and-implementing
-the-presidents-department-of-government-efficiency/.

5 Claire Dickey, "Full List of DOGE Spending Cuts, Findings as Trump Marks One
Month into Second Presidency," Newsweek, February 22, 2025, https://www.newsweek
.com/doge-spending-cuts-findings-one-month-trump-administration-2034150.

6 Stephen Fowler, "Federal Agencies Plan for Mass Layoffs as Trump's Workforce
Cuts Continue," NPR, March 15, 2025, https://www.npr.org/2025/03/15/nx-s1-53
28721/reduction-in-force-rif-federal-workers-job-cuts-musk-doge-layoffs.

7 Danielle Paquette, "Federal Workers Caught in Limbo Amid Trump, DOGE
Efforts to Cut Them," Washington Post, March 8, 2025, https://www.washington
post.com/nation/2025/03/07/federal-workers-firings-legal-unemployment/.

8 Ibid.

9 Korecki, "'You Lose All Hope.'"

10 Michelle Singletary, "Fear, Chaos and Missing Paperwork: DOGE Stories from
Federal Workers," Washington Post, March 19, 2025, https://www.washingtonpost
.com/business/2025/03/19/doge-federal-workers-stories.

11 Korecki, "'You Lose All Hope.'"

12 Ibid.

13 U.S. Environmental Protection Agency, "EPA Launches Biggest Deregulatory
Action in U.S. History," March 14, 2025, https://www.epa.gov/newsreleases/epa
-launches-biggest-deregulatory-action-us-history.

14 Michael Copley, Jeff Brady, and Camila Domonoske, "EPA Announces Dozens
of Environmental Regulations It Plans to Target," NPR, March 12, 2025, https://
www.npr.org/2025/03/12/nx-s1-5326354/trump-epa-environmental-rules-roll
back-deregulation.

15 Ella Nilsen, "Trump Takes an Ax to More Than a Dozen Pollution Rules in Rapid-
Fire Deregulation," March 12, 2025, https://www.cnn.com/2025/03/12/climate
/trump-ev-power-plant-rollbacks.

16 Jean Chemnick and E&E News, "Trump EPA Unveils Aggressive Plans to Dismantle Climate Regulation," Scientific American, March 13, 2025, https://www
.scientificamerican.com/article/trump-epa-unveils-aggressive-plans-to-dismantle
-climate-regulation/.

17 Ellen Knickmeyer, "Unspent Aid Worth Billions Lacks Oversight as Trump Dismantles USAID, Watchdog Warns," Associated Press, February 11, 2025, https://
apnews.com/article/9099c61b33aa7e4bfd40e849853be3b6.

18 Lindsay Whitehurst and Michael Kunzelman, "Judge Rules DOGE's USAID
Dismantling Likely Violates the Constitution," AP News, March 19, 2025,
https://apnews.com/article/usaid-federal-judge-trump-administration-bdc919
a5d98eda5ab72a32fdfe2f147d.

19 Rebecca Kern, "Project 2025 Wanted to Hobble the Federal Workforce. DOGE Has
Hastily Done That, and More," Government Executive, April 9, 2025, https://www
.govexec.com/transition/2025/04/project-2025-wanted-hobble-federal-workforce
-doge-has-hastily-done-and-more/404390/.

20 Korecki, "'You Lose All Hope.'"

21 Brian Witte, "Amid DOGE Cuts, Federal Judge Struggles with Scope of Relief for
Fired Workers," Federal News Network, March 26, 2025, https://federalnews
network.com/litigation/2025/03/federal-judge-struggles-with-scope-of-relief-for
-fired-workers/.

22 Andrea Hsu, "A 2nd Judge Orders Thousands of Fired Federal Employees Temporarily Reinstated," NPR, March 14, 2025, https://www.npr.org/2025/03/13/nx-s1 -5325694/maryland-court-fired-federal-employees-trump.

23 Gary Grumbach, Chloe Atkins, and Nnamdi Egwuonwu, "Judge Orders DOGE Employee to Testify in Lawsuit against the Trump Administration," NBC News, February 28, 2025, https://www.nbcnews.com/politics/doge/judge-orders-doge -employee-testify-lawsuit-trump-administration-rcna194145.

24 Hsu, "A 2nd Judge Orders Thousands of Fired Federal Employees Temporarily Reinstated."

25 Jessica Riedl, "The Actual Math behind DOGE's Cuts," *The Atlantic*, May 8, 2025, https://www.theatlantic.com/politics/archive/2025/05/musk-doge-spending-cuts /682736/.

26 Stephen Fowler, "DOGE Wants to Cut $1 Trillion This Year. But It's Not Looking at Big Spending Drivers," NPR, March 6, 2025, https://www.npr.org/2025/03/06 /nx-s1-5318072/how-much-money-has-doge-saved-budget-deficit-congress.

27 Tim Reid, Helen Coster, and James Oliphant, "Musk's DOGE Cuts Based More on Political Ideology Than Real Cost Savings So Far," Reuters, February 13, 2025, https://www.reuters.com/world/us/musk-cuts-based-more-political-ideology -than-real-cost-savings-so-far-2025-02-12/.

28 Ibid.

29 Avi Asher-Schapiro, Andy Kroll, and Christopher Bing, "DOGE's Millions: As Musk and Trump Gut the Government, Their Ax-Cutting Agency Gets a Cash Infusion," *Government Executive*, February 21, 2025, https://www.govexec.com /management/2025/02/doges-millions-musk-and-trump-gut-government-their -ax-cutting-agency-gets-cash-infusion/403197/.

30 Korecki, "'You Lose All Hope.'"

CHAPTER 10

1 "Ukrainian Human Rights Lawyer Discusses Her Work Exposing Hidden Stories of the War," ABC News, December 11, 2024, https://abcnews.go.com/International /ukrainian-human-rights-lawyer-discusses-work-exposing-hidden/story?id=116 632823.

2 "Center for Civil Liberties, Memorial and Ales Bialiatski—The Nobel Peace Prize 2022," The Nobel Peace Prize, October 7, 2022, https://www.nobelprize.org /educational-nobel-prize-lessons-peace-2022/.

3 Ruth Ben-Ghiat, *Strongmen: Mussolini to the Present* (W.W. Norton & Company, 2020), a theme that repeats throughout the book.

4 "Trump Tells Americans What Putin Wants Them to Hear," *Bloomberg*, April 28, 2025. https://www.bloomberg.com/features/2025-trump-putin-policy/.

5 Veronika Melkozerova "'Crimea Will Stay with Russia,' Trump Tells *Time*," *Politico*, April 25, 2025, https://www.politico.eu/article/donald-trump-crimea-stay-with -russia-ukraine-war/.

6 Mark Trevelyan and Steve Holland, "Trump Says Ukraine Deal Close after Envoy Witkoff Meets Putin," Reuters, April 25, 2025, https://www.reuters.com/world /trumps-envoy-witkoff-arrives-moscow-interfax-reports-2025-04-25/; Keir Simmons, Carol E. Lee, Dan De Luce, and Courtney Kube, "Trump Envoy Relied on Kremlin Interpreter in Meetings with Putin to End War in Ukraine," NBC News, May 10, 2025, https://www.nbcnews.com/world/russia/russia-ukraine-war -trump-envoy-witkoff-interpreter-kremlin-rcna205878.

7   "Trump Praises Xi's 'Extraordinary' Rise," BBC News, October 25, 2017, https://www.bbc.com/news/world-asia-china-41756769.

8   "Many U.S. Companies Plan to Keep China Ties, Survey Finds," *Wall Street Journal*, April 2025, https://www.wsj.com/world/china/many-u-s-companies-plan-to-keep-china-ties-survey-finds-906481c9; William D. Cohen, "The Money Is Too Good to Pass Up: Wall Street Isn't Letting Khashoggi's Killing Get in the Way of Saudi Business," *Vanity Fair*, February 2021, https://www.vanityfair.com/news/2021/02/wall-street-isnt-letting-jamal-khashoggis-killing-get-in-the-way-of-saudi-business. Also, Tyler Kruse, "BP, Shell and Exxon among Top Western Energy Companies Responsible for Almost $100bn Going to Russian Government since 2014 Crimea Invasion," Greenpeace USA, March 25, 2022, https://www.greenpeace.org/usa/bp-shell-and-exxon-among-top-western-energy-companies-responsible-for-almost-100bn-going-to-russian-government-since-2014-crimea-invasion/.

9   Alan Rappeport, "Tillerson's Company, Exxon, Has Billions at Stake over Russia Sanctions," *New York Times*, December 12, 2016, https://www.nytimes.com/2016/12/12/world/europe/rex-tillersons-company-exxon-has-billions-at-stake-over-russia-sanctions.html.

10 Julie Hirschfeld Davis, "Trump, at Putin's Side, Questions U.S. Intelligence on 2016 Election," *New York Times*, July 16, 2018, https://www.nytimes.com/2018/07/16/world/europe/trump-putin-election-intelligence.html.

11 Ibid.

12 Erin Banco, Gram Slattery, and Humeyra Pamuk, "Trump Envoy's Embrace of Russian Demands Worries Republicans, U.S. Allies," Reuters, April 11, 2025, https://www.reuters.com/world/trump-envoys-embrace-russian-demands-worries-republicans-us-allies-2025-04-11/.

13 Shane Harris, Greg Miller, and Josh Dawsey, "CIA Concludes Saudi Crown Prince Ordered Jamal Khashoggi's Assassination," *Washington Post*, November 16, 2018, https://www.washingtonpost.com/world/national-security/cia-concludes-saudi-crown-prince-ordered-jamal-khashoggis-assassination/2018/11/16/98c89fe6-e9b2-11e8-a939-9469f1166f9d_story.html.

14 Bob Woodward, *Rage* (Simon & Schuster, 2020), 212.

15 "Saudi Arabia Plans $600 billion in New US Investment, Trade over Four Years," Reuters, January 22, 2025, https://www.reuters.com/world/middle-east/saudi-crown-prince-seeks-600-bln-investment-push-with-us-2025-01-22/.

16 "US Agrees to Sell Saudi Arabia $142 Billion Arms Package," Reuters, May 13, 2025, https://www.reuters.com/world/us-saudi-arabia-have-discussed-riyadhs-potential-purchase-f-35-jets-2025-05-13/.

17 "Trump Poised to Offer Saudi Arabia over $100 Billion Arms Package, Sources Say," *Economic Times*, April 25, 2025, https://economictimes.indiatimes.com/news/defence/trump-poised-to-offer-saudi-arabia-over-100-billion-arms-package-sources-say/articleshow/120600506.cms.

18 Susannah George, "Saudi Arabia Plays a Crucial Role in Trump's Foreign Policy Ambitions," *Washington Post*, April 2, 2025, https://www.washingtonpost.com/world/2025/04/02/saudi-arabia-trump-foreign-policy/.

19 Joel Schalit, "Trans-Europe Express: Orbán's Trump Fetish Backfires," Euractiv, June 2, 2017, https://www.euractiv.com/section/global-europe/news/trans-europe-express-orbans-trump-fetish-backfires/.

20 Brett Wilkins, "Critics Warn Orbán Visit Aimed at Tutoring Trump on 'How to

Destroy a Democracy,'" Common Dreams, March 8, 2024, https://www.common dreams.org/news/trump-orban.

21 "Trump Says He Still Has Good Relations with Leader of 'Nuclear Power' North Korea," Reuters, March 13, 2025, https://www.reuters.com/world/trump-says-he -still-has-good-relations-with-leader-nuclear-power-north-korea-2025-03-13/.

22 Greg Grandin, Empire's Workshop: Latin America, the United States, and the Making of an Imperial Republic (Metropolitan Books, 2006), 220–227.

23 David Smith, "Golden Trump Statue Turning Heads at CPAC Was Made in Mexico," The Guardian, February 27, 2021, https://www.theguardian.com/us-news /2021/feb/27/golden-trump-statue-mexico-cpac.

24 "Trump and the Middle East, with Steven A. Cook," Council on Foreign Relations, YouTube, November 12, 2024, https://www.youtube.com/watch?v=HPvrFSXQt2I.

25 Sophie Tatum, "Trump Defends Putin: 'You Think Our Country's So Innocent?,'" CNN, February 6, 2017, https://www.cnn.com/2017/02/04/politics/donald-trump -vladimir-putin.

26 Katherine Jacobsen, "Alarm Bells: Trump's First 100 Days Ramp Up Fear for the Press, Democracy," Committee to Protect Journalists Special Report, April 16, 2020, https://cpj.org/special-reports/alarm-bells-trumps-first-100-days -ramp-up-fear-for-the-press-democracy/.

27 Leonard Downie Jr., "The Trump Administration and the Media," Committee to Protect Journalists Special Report, April 30, 2025, https://cpj.org/reports/2020/04 /trump-media-attacks-credibility-leaks/.

28 Lexi Lonas Cochran, "Trump Asked Justice to Look into 'SNL': Report," The Hill, June 22, 2021, https://thehill.com/blogs/blog-briefing-room/news/559588-trump -asked-justice-to-look-into-snl-report/.

29 "A Speech to Europe 2023 by Oleksandra Matviichuk," Institute for Human Sciences, May 9, 2023, https://www.iwm.at/documenting-ukraine/blog/a-speech-to -europe-2023-by-oleksandra-matviichuk.

30 Amenah Elgazzar, "Erosion of Democratic Norm in Trump's America," Democratic Erosion, February 14, 2025, https://democratic-erosion.org/2025/02/14 /erosion-of-democratic-norm-in-trumps-america/.

CHAPTER 11

1 Nadja Popovich, Livia Albeck-Ripka, and Kendra Pierre-Louis, "The Trump Administration Rolled Back More Than 100 Environmental Rules. Here's the Full List," New York Times, January 20, 2021. https://www.nytimes.com/interactive/2020 /climate/trump-environment-rollbacks-list.html.

2 Chris Mooney, and Juliet Eilperin. "EPA Website Removes Climate Science Site from Public View after Two Decades," Washington Post, April 29, 2017. https://www .washingtonpost.com/news/energy-environment/wp/2017/04/28/epa-website -removes-climate-science-site-from-public-view-after-two-decades/; Dina Fine Maron, "Trump Administration Restricts News from Federal Scientists at USDA, EPA." Scientific American, January 2017. https://www.scientificamerican.com/arti cle/trump-administration-restricts-news-from-federal-scientists-at-usda-epa/.

3 Kristina Wong, "Trump Dismisses Climate Change Role in Fires, Says Newsom Needs to Manage Forest Better," The Hill, September 21, 2020, https://the hill.com/homenews/administration/517334-trump-dismisses-climate-change -role-in-fires-says-newsom-needs-to/.

4 Konstantin Toropin and Leah Asmelash, "Oregon Fires: A Young Boy Was Found

Dead with His Dog in His Lap after Trying to Escape Wildfire," CNN, September 12, 2020, https://www.cnn.com/2020/09/11/us/oregon-wildfire-victim-trnd/index .html.

5 Donald J. Trump, "Executive Order on Creating Schedule F in the Excepted Service," White House Archives, October 21, 2020, https://trumpwhitehouse.archives .gov/presidential-actions/executive-order-creating-schedule-f-excepted-service/.

6 "Secretary Bernhardt Signs Record of Decision for Oil Development in ANWR Coastal Plain," Press Release, Bureau of Land Management. August 17, 2020, https://www.doi.gov/pressreleases/secretary-bernhardt-signs-decision-implement -coastal-plain-oil-and-gas-leasing-program.

7 Intergovernmental Panel on Climate Change, *Climate Change 2021: The Physical Science Basis. Contribution of Working Group I to the Sixth Assessment Report of the Intergovernmental Panel on Climate Change* (Cambridge University Press, 2021), https://www.ipcc.ch/report/ar6/wg1/.

8 Adam R. Pearson, Jonathon P. Schuldt, Rainer Romero-Canyas, Matthew T. Ballew, and Dylan Larson-Konar, "Diverse Segments of the US Public Underestimate the Environmental Concerns of Minority and Low-Income Americans," *Proceedings of the National Academy of Sciences* 115, no. 49 (December 2018): 12429–12434, https://www.pnas.org/doi/10.1073/pnas.1804698115.

9 Gabe Cohen, "'We're Not Preparing': As Trump Officials Vow to Eliminate FEMA, the Agency Is Already in Turmoil," CNN, March 26, 2025, https://www.cnn.com /2025/03/26/politics/fema-payments-staffing-stalled-turmoil.

10 Intergovernmental Panel on Climate Change. *Global Warming of 1.5°C. An IPCC Special Report on the Impacts of Global Warming of 1.5°C Above Pre-industrial Levels and Related Global Greenhouse Gas Emission Pathways, in the Context of Strengthening the Global Response to the Threat of Climate Change, Sustainable Development, and Efforts to Eradicate Poverty* (World Meteorological Organization, 2018), https://www.ipcc.ch/sr15/.

PART IV

1 Trump Executive Order "Ending Taxpayer Subsidization of Biased Media," May 1, 2025, https://www.whitehouse.gov/presidential-actions/2025/05/ending-taxpayer -subsidization-of-biased-media/.

2 Patrick Smith and Gary Grumbach, "Trump Signs Executive Order to Stop Federal Funding For NPR and PBS," May 2, 2025, https://www.nbcnews.com/politics /trump-administration/trump-signs-executive-order-stop-federal-funding-npr -pbs-rcna204375.

CHAPTER 12

1 Steve Holland, "Trump Signs Orders Targeting Two Ex-Officials Who Criticized Him," Reuters, April 9, 2025, https://www.reuters.com/world/us/trump-signs -orders-targeting-two-ex-officials-who-criticized-him-2025-04-09/.

2 "Joint Statement from Elections Infrastructure Government Coordinating Council and the Election Infrastructure Sector Coordinating Executive Committees," press release, Cybersecurity & Infrastructure Security Agency, November 12, 2020, https://www.cisa.gov/news-events/news/joint-statement-elections-infrastructure -government-coordinating-council-election-infrastructure.

3 Sam Sabin, "Trump Orders Investigations into 2 DHS Officials from His First Term," Axios, April 10, 2025, https://www.axios.com/2025/04/09/chris-krebs-miles -taylor-doj-investigation-trump.

4 Kim Lane Scheppele, "How Viktor Orbán Wins," *Journal of Democracy* 33, no. 3 (July 2022): 45–60, https://www.journalofdemocracy.org/articles/how-viktor -orban-wins/.

5 "Trump Speaks at CPAC 2023 Transcript," March 4, 2023, https://www.rev.com /transcripts/trump-speaks-at-cpac-2023-transcript.

6 Jamie Gangel, Jeremy Herb, Marshall Cohen, Elizabeth Stuart, and Barbara Starr, "'They're Not Going to F**King Succeed': Top Generals Feared Trump Would Attempt a Coup after Election, According to New Book," CNN, July 14, 2021, https://www.cnn.com/2021/07/14/politics/donald-trump-election-coup-new-book -excerpt/index.html.

7 William Brangham and Harry Zahn, "The Project 2025 Policies the Trump Admin- istration Is Already Implementing," *PBS NewsHour*, February 22, 2025, https:// www.pbs.org/newshour/show/the-project-2025-policies-the-trump-administra tion-is-already-implementing; Jonathan Blitzer, "Inside the Trump Plan for 2025," *New Yorker*, July 15, 2024, https://www.newyorker.com/magazine/2024/07/22/inside -the-trump-plan-for-2025; Robert P. Beschel Jr., "DOGE Was Bad. Schedule F Will Be Worse," *The Atlantic*, April 28, 2025, https://www.theatlantic.com/ideas/archive /2025/04/trump-civil-service-schedule-f/682609/.

8 Perry Stein, "Tracking the Trump Criminal Cases and Where They Stand," *Wash- ington Post*, January 27, 2025. https://www.washingtonpost.com/national-security /2025/01/27/doj-firings-trump-jack-smith-officials/.

9 Brianna Seid, "Project 2025's Plan for Criminal Justice under Trump," Brennan Center for Justice, January 29, 2025, https://www.brennancenter.org/our-work /analysis-opinion/project-2025s-plan-criminal-justice-under-trump.

10 Ken Dilanian and Ryan J. Reilly, "Trump Administration Fires DOJ Officials Who Worked on Criminal Investigations of the President," NBC News, January 28, 2025, https://www.nbcnews.com/politics/justice-department/trump-administration -fires-doj-officials-worked-criminal-investigation-rcna189512.

11 Perry Stein, "DOJ Fires Officials Who Worked on Jack Smith's Trump Investigation," *Washington Post*, January 28, 2025, https://www.washingtonpost.com/national -security/2025/01/27/doj-firings-trump-jack-smith-officials/.

12 "Voting Laws Roundup: December 2024," Brennan Center for Justice, January 15, 2025, https://www.brennancenter.org/our-work/research-reports/voting-laws-round up-2024-review.

13 Morgan Chalfant, "Trump: 'The Only Way We're Going to Lose This Election Is If the Election Is Rigged.'" *The Hill*, August 17, 2023. https://thehill.com/homenews/ad ministration/512424-trump-the-only-way-we-are-going-to-lose-this-election-is -if-the/.

14 Chris Megarian, "Trump Says He's Considering Ways to Serve a Third Term as President," Associated Press, March 30, 2025, https://apnews.com/article /trump-third-term-constitution-22nd-amendment-efba31be02ee96b0ef68b17fe89 7578.

15 Sonam Sheth, "Republican Senator Breaks with JD Vance over Supreme Court," *Newsweek*, February 11, 2025. https://www.newsweek.com/republican-senator -breaks-jd-vance-supreme-court-trump-2029658.

16 Marianne LeVine, "Trump Calls Political Enemies 'Vermin,' Echoing Dictators Hitler, Mussolini," *Washington Post*, November 12, 2023, https://www.washington post.com/politics/2023/11/12/trump-rally-vermin-political-opponents/.

17 Zack Beauchamp, "Viktor Orbán Laid Out His Dark Worldview to the American

Right—and They Loved It," *Vox*, August 5, 2022, https://www.vox.com/2022/8/5/23292448/orban-cpac-dallas-2022-speech-trump.

18 Scheppele, "How Viktor Orbán Wins."

19 Timothy Snyder, *On Tyranny: Twenty Lessons from the Twentieth Century* (Tim Duggan Books, 2017).

20 Kim Lane Scheppele, "Hungary's Illiberal Turn: Disabling the Constitution," *Journal of Democracy* 23, no. 3 (July 2012): 138–145, https://www.journalofdemocracy.org/articles/hungarys-illiberal-turn-disabling-the-constitution/.

21 Kim Lane Scheppele, "The Playbook for American Autocracy" (interview), *The Atlantic*, March 2022, https://www.theatlantic.com/international/archive/2024/07/why-special-republican-relationship-hungary-so-worrying/679035/.

22 "Who Loses When Trump Cuts Funding to Universities?," *Consider This*, NPR, April 2, 2025, https://www.npr.org/2025/04/02/1242229717/who-loses-when-trump-cuts-funding-to-universities.

23 Liam Reilly, "Trump's FCC Is Investigating NPR and PBS Stations over Sponsorships," CNN, January 30, 2025, https://www.cnn.com/2025/01/30/media/trump-fcc-npr-pbs.

24 Spencer Woodman, "The IRS Unit That Audits Billionaires Has Lost 38 percent of Its Employees Since January, New Data Shows," International Consortium of Investigative Journalists, March 28, 2025, https://www.icij.org/news/2025/03/the-irs-unit-that-audits-billionaires-has-lost-38-percent-of-its-employees-since-january-new-data-shows/.

25 Joe Lancaster, "Trump Flagrantly Targets Political Opponents in Executive Orders," Reason, April 14, 2025, https://reason.com/2025/04/14/trump-flagrantly-targets-political-opponents-in-executive-orders/.

26 Katie Stallard, "One Hundred Days of Autocracy," *The New Statesman*, April 29, 2025, https://www.newstatesman.com/international-politics/2025/04/one-hundred-days-of-autocracy.

Chapter 13

1 David Sharp, "Trump Once Again Wants to Cut Energy Assistance to the Poor," Associated Press, February 18, 2018, https://apnews.com/national-national-general-news-3218910423c3415ba4dba6a6a5b25dbb.

2 "The Criminal System Is Full of People with Psychopathy. It Fails to Help Them," Yale University Mechanisms of Disinhibition (MoD) Laboratory, February 27, 2023, https://modlab.yale.edu/news/criminal-system-full-people-psychopathy-it-fails-help-them-appeal; Ana Sanz-García, Clara Gesteira, Jesús Sanz, and María Paz García-Vera, "Prevalence of Psychopathy in the General Adult Population: A Systematic Review and Meta-Analysis," *Frontiers in Psychology* (August 5, 2021), doi: 10.3389/fpsyg.2021.661044; https://pmc.ncbi.nlm.nih.gov/articles/PMC8374040/; Ted Bauer, "So, Are Most CEOs Sociopaths?," The Context of Things, October 17, 2019, https://thecontextofthings.com/2019/10/17/so-are-most-ceos-sociopaths/.

3 Gabriel Sherman, "'Stephen Actually Enjoys Seeing Those Pictures at the Border': The West Wing Is Fracturing over Trump's Callous Migrant-Family Policy," *Vanity Fair*, June 20, 2018, https://www.vanityfair.com/news/2018/06/stephen-miller-family-separation-white-house.

CHAPTER 14

1 Sun-Chul Kim, "South Korea's Candlelight Revolution: The Power of Plaza Democracy," discussed in Alexis Dudden, "Revolution by Candlelight: How South Koreans Toppled a Government," *Dissent Magazine*, October 23, 2017, https://www.dissentmagazine.org/article/revolution-by-candlelight-how-south-koreans-toppled-a-government/.

2 "Chile's 1988 Plebiscite and the End of Pinochet's Dictatorship," Association for Diplomatic Studies and Training, https://adst.org/2014/11/chiles-1988-plebiscite-and-the-end-of-pinochets-dictatorship/.

3 Neil DeVotta, "Sri Lanka's Agony," *Journal of Democracy* 33, no. 3 (July 2022): 92–99, https://www.journalofdemocracy.org/articles/sri-lankas-agony/.

4 Timothy Snyder, "On Tyranny: Twenty Lessons from the Twentieth Century," January 6, 2024, https://snyder.substack.com/p/on-tyranny.

5 "Poland: Freedom in the World 2024 Country Report," Freedom House, 2024, accessed April 29, 2025, https://freedomhouse.org/country/poland/freedom-world/2024.

6 Richard Bernstein, "The Illuminations of Hannah Arendt," *New York Times*, June 20, 2018, https://www.nytimes.com/2018/06/20/opinion/why-read-hannah-arendt-now.html.

7 Justice Louis D. Brandeis, dissenting opinion in New State Ice Co. v. Liebmann, 285 U.S. 262 (1932), https://supreme.justia.com/cases/federal/us/285/262/.

8 Michelle Nicholasen, "Nonviolent Resistance Proves Potent Weapon," *Harvard Gazette*, February 4, 2019, https://news.harvard.edu/gazette/story/2019/02/why-nonviolent-resistance-beats-violent-force-in-effecting-social-political-change/.

9 Bayard Rustin's famous quote "The only weapon we have is our bodies, and we need to tuck them in places so wheels don't turn" is widely cited across multiple platforms. https://quotefancy.com/bayard-rustin-quotes.

10 Maria Popova, "The Great Czech Playwright Turned Dissident Turned President Václav Havel on Hope," The Marginalian, https://www.themarginalian.org/2019/09/22/vaclav-havel-hope/.

11 Justice John Paul Stevens, dissenting opinion in Citizens United v. Federal Election Commission, 558 U.S. 310 (2010), https://supreme.justia.com/cases/federal/us/558/310/#tab-opinion-1963047.

12 Rose Deller, "Book Review: *Dark Money: The Hidden History of the Billionaires behind the Rise of the Radical Right* by Jane Mayer," *LSE Review of Books*, March 20, 2017, https://blogs.lse.ac.uk/lsereviewofbooks/2017/03/20/book-review-dark-money-the-hidden-history-of-the-billionaires-behind-the-rise-of-the-radical-right-by-jane-mayer/.

13 Martin Gilens and Benjamin I. Page, "Testing Theories of American Politics: Elites, Interest Groups, and Average Citizens," *Perspectives on Politics* 12, no. 3 (2014): 564–581, https://doi.org/10.1017/S1537592714001595.

14 "Lobbying Data Summary," OpenSecrets.org, accessed April 2024, https://www.opensecrets.org/federal-lobbying.

15 Mariame Kaba, "Hope Is a Discipline," interview by Brian Sonenstein and Kim Wilson, *Beyond Prisons Podcast*, Episode 19, published by Toward Freedom, September 16, 2020, https://towardfreedom.org/story/archives/activism/hope-is-a-discipline/.

16 Discussed in numerous articles about judicial politics: Amanda Hollis-Brusky, "Ideas with Consequences: The Federalist Society and the Conservative Counter-revolution," American Constitution Society, March 16, 2015, https://www.acslaw.org/book/ideas-with-consequences-the-federalist-society-and-the-conservative-counterrevolution/.

17 Senator Sheldon Whitehouse, "The Scheme: How the Right Wing Used Dark Money to Capture the Supreme Court," YouTube, https://www.youtube.com/playlist?list=PLhyg5hj7I21i1Aqcaym9TRFrpWjPN9_ms.

18 Jennifer Heerwig and Brian J. McCabe, "Building a More Diverse Donor Coalition: An Analysis of the Seattle Democracy Voucher Program in the 2019 Election Cycle," McCourt School of Public Policy, Georgetown University, December 16, 2020, https://mccourt.georgetown.edu/news/building-a-more-diverse-donor-coalition/.

19 Robert W. McChesney, *The Political Economy of Media: Enduring Issues, Emerging Dilemmas* (Monthly Review Press, 2008).

20 Jamie Gangel, Jeremy Herb, and Elizabeth Stuart, "Exclusive: Retired Republican Judge Says January 6 Was 'Well-Developed Plan' by Trump to Cling to Power," CNN, June 16, 2022, https://www.cnn.com/2022/06/16/politics/luttig-statement-trump-plan-january-6-committee.

21 Nicole Winfield, "Pope Leo XIV Lays Out Vision of Papacy and Identifies AI as a Main Challenge for Humanity," AP News, May 10, 2025, https://apnews.com/article/pope-leo-vision-papacy-artificial-intelligence-36d29e37a11620b594b9b7c0574cc358.

22 Raluca Csernatoni, "Can Democracy Survive the Disruptive Power of AI?," Carnegie Endowment for International Peace, December 18, 2024, https://carnegieendowment.org/research/2024/12/can-democracy-survive-the-disruptive-power-of-ai.

23 George Santayana's famous quote "'Those who cannot remember the past are condemned to repeat it" is from *The Life of Reason* (1905), preserved by the Santayana Edition: The Works of George Santayana, https://santayana.indianapolis.iu.edu/about-santayana/santayana-quotations/.

24 Jelani Cobb has discussed historical memory and race in multiple interviews and writings for the *New Yorker* and other platforms, including appearances on NPR, "In *The Matter of Black Lives*, Generations of Black Thinkers Probe American Racism," October 22, 2021, https://www.npr.org/2021/10/22/1048421433/in-the-matter-of-black-lives-generations-of-black-thinkers-probe-american-racism.

25 Elie Wiesel, Nobel Peace Prize Acceptance Speech, December 10, 1986, https://www.nobelprize.org/prizes/peace/1986/wiesel/acceptance-speech/.

26 Kaba, "Hope Is a Discipline."

EPILOGUE

1 Presidential Recordings Program, Miller Center, University of Virginia, "Conversation with Sen. Everett Dirksen," October 31, 1968, https://millercenter.org/the-presidency/educational-resources/this-is-treason.

2 Peter Baker and Nick Corasaniti, "Former Texas Politician Says He Participated in Iran Hostage Negotiations," *New York Times*, March 18, 2023, https://www.nytimes.com/2023/03/18/us/politics/jimmy-carter-october-surprise-iran-hostages.html.

3 David Johnson, "Bush Pardons 6 in Iran Affair, Aborting a Weinberger Trial; Prosecutor Assails 'Cover-Up,'" *New York Times*, December 25, 1992, https://www.nytimes.com/1992/12/25/us/pardons-bush-pardons-6-iran-affair-aborting-weinberger-trial-prosecutor-assails.html.

4 Jeffrey Toobin, *Too Close to Call: The Thirty-Six-Day Battle to Decide the 2000 Election* (Random House, 2001).

5 Greg Palast, *The Best Democracy Money Can Buy: The Truth about Corporate Cons, Globalization, and High-Finance Fraudsters* (Plume, 2004).

6 Carol Anderson, *One Person, No Vote: How Voter Suppression Is Destroying Our Democracy* (Bloomsbury Publishing, 2018).

7 Robert S. Mueller, "Report on the Investigation into Russian Interference in the 2016 Presidential Election," U.S. Department of Justice, 2019, https://www.justice.gov/archives/sco/file/1373816/download.

Acknowledgments

At Berrett-Koehler Publishers, special thanks go to Jeevan Sivasubramaniam (who has helped keep me sane for years) and Neal Maillet, a constant source of encouragement and wisdom. BK is an extraordinary publishing company, and it's been an honor to have them publish my books for almost two decades. And thanks to Tai Moses, who edited *The Thom Hartmann Reader* and returned to do a first pass with this book, for all her insights and help. BK also provided an experienced copyeditor for the book, Cathy Mallon, who smoothed and tightened the text.

Index

About the Author

Thom Hartmann is the *New York Times* best-selling, four-time Project Censored award-winning, author of more than forty books, of which more than thirty are currently in print. He publishes a daily Substack newsletter about politics, *The Hartmann Report,* that's available at hartmannreport.com and has more than 165,000 subscribers.

Thom has also been the nation's number one progressive talk show host for more than two decades, having written the original business plan for Air America Radio in 2003, when he started his program. He's live daily from noon to 3 p.m. EST on commercial radio stations all across the United States, on non-profit stations via the Pacifica Network, and on channel 127 of the SiriusXM Satellite radio network. The program is also simulcast as TV via the Free Speech TV Network, carried on DISH and DirectTV satellite networks, Hulu, Apple TV, Sling, cable systems nationwide, on the internet at freespeech.org, and on every major social media platform including X, Bluesky, Substack, Twitch, TikTok, YouTube, and Facebook. His show's website is thom.tv.

Thom also cowrote, narrated, and/or was featured in seven movies and documentaries with Leonardo DiCaprio, including *The 11th Hour, Ice On Fire, Last Hours, Carbon,* and others. Most are now available on various streaming platforms.

As an entrepreneur, Thom has also founded several successful businesses, including two advertising agencies, an herbal tea company, and an international wholesale travel business. Thom has lived and worked with his wife, Louise, and their three children on several continents. Thom was born (1951) and grew up in Michigan, and retains strong ties to the Midwest, although he and Louise have lived in New Hampshire, Vermont,

209

Georgia, Washington, DC, and Germany. Thom and Louise now live with a small menagerie of cats, dogs, geese, river otters, and ducks on the Columbia River near Portland, Oregon.

Recent books authored by Thom Hartmann include the following:

The Hidden History of the American Dream: The Demise of the Middle Class—and How to Rescue Our Future

The Hidden History of American Democracy: Rediscovering Humanity's Ancient Way of Living

The Hidden History of Big Brother in America: How the Death of Privacy and the Rise of Surveillance Threaten Us and Our Democracy

The Hidden History of Neoliberalism: How Reaganism Gutted America and How to Restore Its Greatness

The Hidden History of American Oligarchy: Reclaiming Our Democracy from the Ruling Class

The Hidden History of American Healthcare: Why Sickness Bankrupts You and Makes Others Insanely Rich

The Hidden History of Monopolies: How Big Business Destroyed the American Dream

The Hidden History of the War on Voting: Who Stole Your Vote—and How to Get It Back

The Hidden History of the Supreme Court and the Betrayal of America

The Hidden History of Guns and the Second Amendment

Berrett–Koehler
Publishers

Berrett-Koehler is an independent publisher dedicated to an ambitious mission: *Connecting people and ideas to create a world that works for all.*

Our publications span many formats, including print, digital, audio, and video. We also offer online resources, training, and gatherings. And we will continue expanding our products and services to advance our mission.

We believe that the solutions to the world's problems will come from all of us, working at all levels: in our society, in our organizations, and in our own lives. Our publications and resources offer pathways to creating a more just, equitable, and sustainable society. They help people make their organizations more humane, democratic, diverse, and effective (and we don't think there's any contradiction there). And they guide people in creating positive change in their own lives and aligning their personal practices with their aspirations for a better world.

And we strive to practice what we preach through what we call "The BK Way." At the core of this approach is *stewardship,* a deep sense of responsibility to administer the company for the benefit of all of our stakeholder groups, including authors, customers, employees, investors, service providers, sales partners, and the communities and environment around us. Everything we do is built around stewardship and our other core values of *quality, partnership, inclusion,* and *sustainability.*

We are grateful to our readers, authors, and other friends who are supporting our mission. We ask you to share with us examples of how BK publications and resources are making a difference in your lives, organizations, and communities at bkconnection.com/impact.

Dear reader,

Thank you for picking up this book and welcome to the worldwide BK community! You're joining a special group of people who have come together to create positive change in their lives, organizations, and communities.

What's BK all about?

Our mission is to connect people and ideas to create a world that works for all.

Why? Our communities, organizations, and lives get bogged down by old paradigms of self-interest, exclusion, hierarchy, and privilege. But we believe that can change. That's why we seek the leading experts on these challenges—and share their actionable ideas with you.

A welcome gift

To help you get started, we'd like to offer you a **free copy** of one of our bestselling ebooks:

bkconnection.com/welcome

When you claim your **free ebook**, you'll also be subscribed to our blog.

Our freshest insights

Access the best new tools and ideas for leaders at all levels on our blog at ideas.bkconnection.com.

Sincerely,

Your friends at Berrett-Koehler

MIX
Paper | Supporting
responsible forestry
FSC
www.fsc.org   FSC® C005010